ABC

Practical Guide to Dog Training

STEVEN APPELBAUM

HOWELL
BOOK
HOUSE

To my loving hound dog Buford. Thank you for reaffirming
the importance of patience and loving-kindness. Also, for
proving that unconditional love does exist.

This book is printed on acid-free paper. ∞

Copyright © 2004 by Wiley Publishing, Inc. All rights reserved

Howell Book House
Published by Wiley Publishing, Inc., Hoboken, New Jersey
Published simultaneously in Canada

All photos not otherwise credited are provided by the author.

For general information about our other products and services, please contact our Customer Care Department within the United States at (800) 762-2974, outside the United States at (317) 572-3993 or fax (317) 572-4002.

Wiley also publishes its books in a variety of electronic formats. Some content that appears in print may not be available in electronic books. For more information about Wiley products, visit our web site at www.wiley.com.

Library of Congress Cataloging-in-Publication Data:
Appelbaum, Steven.
  ABC practical guide to dog training / Steven Appelbaum.
    p. cm.
  ISBN 0-7645-6722-5 (alk. paper)
  1. Dogs—Training. I. Title.
  SF431.A66 2004
  636.7'0887—dc22

                                            2003015628

Printed in the United States of America

10 9 8 7 6 5 4

CONTENTS

PREFACE

As any visit to a book store or pet supply store will confirm, there are dozens of books about dog training. With the proliferation of titles, the question "Why another book on dog training?" needs to be asked.

The answer—or rather, answers—to that question are varied. First, many dog training books are written by trainers who are looking to create name recognition for themselves. Others are looking to impress colleagues, especially if these trainers want to pursue seminar or speaking careers. Then there are those who are tired of training and hope to make a living as writers. While there is nothing inherently wrong with any of these motives, I think they miss what I believe must be the primary motive for anyone who is writing a serious book on training: that any such book must first and foremost be written for dog owners who are looking for answers about how to properly train their pets.

In my experience, dog owners are looking for answers that are humane and that work. This book is dedicated to them. I didn't write *ABC Practical Guide to Dog Training* to win points with other trainers, nor did I write it to build my business. Instead, I wrote it because I am very passionate about certain things.

Shelter and rescue organizations throughout North America will confirm the fact that at least 60 percent of all dogs in shelters are there because of untreated behavior problems. They will also confirm, as will many veterinarians, that millions of dogs are killed in shelters every year. This makes untreated behavior problems the largest preventable cause of death of pet dogs in North America. That's an appalling statistic. As a trainer, it seems logical to me that a training message based on methods that work needs to be shared with the public, and what better way than a book?

This book is not for everyone. While the methods I have described are strongly focused on using rewards, I make no bones about the fact that correction sometimes has a place in the training process.

It used to be that dog training was almost always based on compulsion. This means the dog learned to listen primarily to avoid some sort of correction or punishment. The problem with these techniques is that the physical punishment was sometimes emotionally and physically damaging to the dog. Anyone who took a training class 25 or more years ago will remember just how rough training classes could be.

We have made tremendous and exciting advances in the last decade or so. Over time, a new attitude and understanding were embraced by trainers. Instead of teaching the dog to avoid punishment based on what she shouldn't do, trainers focused on strongly rewarding appropriate behavior. Correction was administered only after the dog had clearly learned a desired response and decided at that point to disobey. These methods are far more positive and are extremely effective. Today, greater numbers of trainers have a stronger understanding about the scientific principles of how dogs learn than ever before. Additionally, modern methods based on the proper use of rewards can be incredibly effective.

But now, some trainers believe any physical correction is cruel and unnecessary. Rather than debate that point with them, I decided to write this book and share tried, true and tested techniques that work. This, more than anything, is what will keep dogs out of shelters and strengthen the bond between owners and their pets.

ABC Practical Guide to Dog Training is very user-friendly. It focuses on what you, a dog owner, can do starting the very first day you bring your dog home. The book explains what commonly used behavioral terms really mean, explains "pack theory" in a way that makes sense, delves into ways you can humanely and effectively address behavior problems such as jumping, nipping, chewing, house soiling, digging, barking and much more. The book also teaches you how to train your dog off leash, and where and how you can find the best dog trainers. It ends with an Internet guide to numerous sites devoted to all things doggy, including sites about canine behavior, pet supplies, locating trainers, dog parks, boarding kennels, pet-friendly locations of every conceivable type, schools for dog trainers, veterinarians, dog books and magazines, and more. There's even a dog law site and resource guide for those readers who, after reading this book, are so inspired that they wish to become trainers themselves.

ACKNOWLEDGMENTS

The Monks of New Skete said it best when they said, "No one ever learns in a vacuum." In truth, all good teachers learn as they instruct. That being said, I start off by thanking all of my students, both two-legged and four-legged. Thank you for putting up with my imperfections and being open enough to learn and teach. Special thanks to an amazing trainer and human being, Debbie Kendrick—we have watched each other grow for 15 years. Without her I wouldn't be here. Kristyne Bennett, without whom I would never have been able to write this book. The entire staff at ABTA, including but not limited to Sandy Novotny, Sarah Drain and Candace Kendrick. Marc Appelbaum, even though I don't always say it, you make me proud. The entire staff of Animal Behavior College, a truly amazing group. William Campbell, whose training philosophy changed my direction. Richard Wolters, whose training philosophy started me on the path. Pet business people: Bill Lechtner, Randy Boyd, Mike Woodard, Stu Wolman, Paul Jolly, Kathi Hoffman-Weiner, Michael Steinberg, Joel Silverman and numerous others whom I have had the pleasure to know and work with over the years. Ian Dunbar, Karen Pryor, Pamela Reid, Martin and Pat Deeley, William Koehler, Job Michael Evans and dozens of others from across the ideological spectrum, some of whom I know, some of whom I've read and all of whom I've learned from. Mom, Dad, Richard, Beth, Sybil, Lyn, Diane, Taffy Stern and Karen and Kristi Lewis, all of whom have loved me through everything.

About the Author

Steven Appelbaum is the President and CEO of Animal Behavior and Training Associates, Inc., the largest independent dog training company in North America. ABTA offers dog training classes in 47 states and five Canadian provinces. It employs more than 500 trainers. In 2002, ABTA had well over 25,000 students in its training programs. Appelbaum is also the President and Interim Director of Animal Behavior College, Inc. (ABC). This highly innovative school for professional dog trainers has students in all 50 states and Canada. With graduating class totals of more than 400 in 2002, ABC is helping to train the next generation of dog trainers. Steve also does consulting for pet product vendors and manufacturers, and has had several articles published in *Off Lead* magazine. He is currently on the Board of Directors of the International Association of Canine Professionals. He lives in Los Angeles with Buford, whom he considers to be the world's cutest Basset Hound. This is his first book.

CHAPTER 1

A DOG STORY

I am a professional dog trainer and have been one since 1980. I started my business by drawing a flyer (I always fancied myself a bit of an artist), making copies and posting them on bulletin boards in local markets around the San Fernando Valley in North Los Angeles. The first month in business I got 10 customers using this technique, and from that day forward I worked as a full-time trainer. Looking back, I cringe at what I thought I knew and, with the perspective of time, what I didn't know.

Like most of you reading this book, I've always had a deep, passionate love of animals in general and dogs in particular. This was true at a very young age. One of my earliest memories is walking down the street and having a large German Shepherd Dog come running up to me. The dog, whose face was just about even with mine (I was six at the time), sniffed me, and I happily let him while I scratched his side. Thirty-seven years later, I can still see his leg going thump, thump, thump on the sidewalk as I scratched a nice, sensitive spot on his body. He then proceeded to lick my face. I have always loved doggie kisses and I was just out there enough, even then, that I probably licked him back.

Our beginning love affair was interrupted by the dog's owner, who came running out of the house shouting at me, "Don't move!," while he grabbed his dog. He sternly ordered me to stay where I was and disappeared into the backyard, dog in tow. A minute or so later he came back out and carefully checked me to make sure his dog hadn't bitten or injured me in any way. He asked me if I was all right. I was scared at this point and only remember nodding yes. He asked my name and told me to go home. That evening he called my parents and suggested that I ought to learn not to pet strange dogs. My parents talked to me about this and I recall saying, "But the dog came up and petted me." I remember my mom looking at me a bit strangely (not the first time or the last), and the matter was dropped.

I learned later that this dog had bitten half a dozen people, including a small girl. The dog was later euthanized. I didn't hear of this for several years, but I vividly recall the feeling of absolute sadness when I heard this news. In truth, as I write this I still feel a little sad. Dogs and I have always had a special kind of bond.

As a child growing up on Long Island, New York, we had a large female Weimaraner named Misty. She was sweet, hyper, totally

Steve at age six.

I enjoyed rubbing Misty's belly
almost as much as I liked chasing
her around the neighborhood.

disobedient and liked nothing better than to blast out of the house and run around the neighborhood, often with half a dozen kids trying to catch her. One day a few friends and I had the brilliant idea that we could lasso her. We had to test this, and unbeknownst to my parents, on a couple of occasions I deliberately let her out so that we could chase her on our bicycles, throwing ropes in her direction. Given that there weren't a lot of people in the late 1960s on Long Island with roping experience, or at least none who offered to teach my friends and me, we never did succeed in catching her that way. This was undoubtedly a good thing.

When Misty was about a year and a half old, my mom finally convinced my dad to take Misty to obedience school. The classes took place on Saturday mornings at 10 a.m. at a local park. I remember going to class the second week. There were 10 or 12 other dog owners with a variety of dogs. I don't recall all the breeds, although I do distinctly remember a couple of German Shepherds, a Cocker Spaniel and at least two Irish Setters. All of the handlers were men, and there were three other kids about my age in attendance, as well. The instructor, a man who seemed ancient at the time but was probably in his early 40s, had a crew cut and a very well trained Boxer. All the dogs were at least six months old, with most closer to a year or older. All the dogs were on choke chains, except for one who was on what I later learned was a pinch collar.

The trainer was working on teaching the class how to properly "heel" their dogs. I learned that "heel" meant the dog walked next to you at your left side, even if you sped up, slowed down or turned around. Most dogs in this class tended to pull ahead, which the trainer called "forging." To correct the forging behavior, the trainer instructed the handlers to immediately turn in the opposite direction and literally run the other way. Since most of the dogs were big, the kids couldn't participate in this exercise. I will never forget seeing what happened when a 60-pound dog wearing a metal choke chain attached to a leash held by a 180-pound man goes in one direction and the man runs in the other. I saw dogs completely flipped off their feet, screaming, yelping and, to be honest, more than a few learning very quickly not to forge ahead.

After "teaching" this for about 15 minutes, the trainer separated the class and had half walk about 50 feet away and face the other half. The trainer then instructed the first group to heel their dogs toward the second group, which was ordered to remain still. Any forgers were quickly dealt with. When the moving group got about 15 feet from the stationary group, a man's dog in the stationary group started barking at one of the dogs moving toward them. This dog then lunged forward, dragging his handler toward the other dogs.

The trainer moved quickly to the offending dog, took the leash and sharply jerked it in an attempt to correct the barking, lunging behavior. When this had no effect, the trainer shouted "No" and repeated the correction more strongly. It's funny what things become etched in your mind. I remember like it was yesterday watching the dog's paws leave the ground as the trainer yanked the leash. The dog turned toward the

Dad at 35.

trainer, and the trainer, perhaps thinking this dog was going to bite him, completely lifted the animal off the ground and held him dangling in the air. The dog's barks became strangled yelps, and after 10 or 15 seconds of struggling, the dog just kind of went limp. The trainer then put the dog back on the ground, snapped the leash once more for good measure and handed the leash back to his owner. The dog just kind of stood there, still conscious but clearly dazed. I vividly remember wishing I were old enough and strong enough to put the trainer on a leash and collar and treat him exactly the same way. Great lessons for a kid to learn, huh?

To his credit, my dad was sensitive enough to recognize that this type of "training experience" was not appropriate for his 10-year-old son. This was my first introduction to the world of dog training. My dad and dog went back for a few more classes without me and then they both became doggie school dropouts. We never did get Misty trained, which never bothered me in the least. I liked chasing her.

As I grew older, my interest in animals grew, as did my passion for dogs. I know I must have watched *The Incredible Journey* at least a hundred times before I was 12. I started reading about dogs and about training. Most books on the subject were tough going for a kid, but a few stood out. One in particular, a book written in the early 1960s called *Family Dog* by Richard Wolters, was a favorite. This book advocated some things considered very radical at the time, including doing a good deal of obedience training with puppies much younger than six months of age. Wolters' methods were also considerably gentler than a lot of others out there at the time—although still fairly rough by today's standards. In fact, many of the pictures in this book showed the author's young daughter doing a lot of the training. He also discussed canine developmental periods and suggested many of the ideas that are taken for granted now, 40 years later. I often wondered whatever happened to his daughter and whether the author ever knew how many people his books influenced.

For many years I considered becoming a veterinarian, but was very unsure that I would ever be able to euthanize a single animal. By the time I was 20, I had probably read 80 or 90 books on the subject of behavior and training. I also attended a number of training schools and had decided to become a professional trainer. My reasons were varied, but certainly included the fact that I could help dogs, as well as play with them, and get paid for it. Imagine getting paid to be with puppies. How cool is that? I thought it was extremely cool, and although the trials and tribulations of building, managing and promoting two nationally recognized training organizations can, at times, be anything but cool, the truth is I still get paid to play with puppies!

I have always maintained a pragmatic and open mind toward training methods, recognizing that truly open-minded people don't think they know it all. I've always been aware that the day I felt I knew it all would be the day I would cease to learn. Since I've always wanted to learn about dogs, I've always been very clear that I don't come close to knowing all there is. What I do know is that I would never be like the trainer I remembered from my youth. Not ever!

In my travels, I learned that positive reward-based training is almost always more effective than training based on punishment. However, correction does have a place, as does reward, good timing and excellent communication in the training process. Very critically, I've learned to remain sensitive and loving toward my four-legged students, and even most of my two-legged ones.

In my 20-plus years as a professional trainer, I have found that my clients want specific things when dealing with behavior problems in their pets:

◆ First, they want methods that do not cause harm to the dog.

◆ Second, they want methods that WORK.

This last point is a key one. If a method doesn't work, the problem continues. Often if a problem continues, owners will abandon or rehome their dogs. I have heard veterinarians say untreated behavior problems are the largest preventable cause of death of companion dogs in the United States. I believe this, and any trip to a local animal shelter will confirm the fact that a large percentage of dogs in shelters are there due to untreated behavior problems. The tragic part is that most behavior problems can be dealt with, especially if you start right away.

Using modern, scientific methods, trainers and owners can now more effectively and humanely address behavioral challenges than ever before. Unfortunately, many trainers and owners have fallen victim to a type of thinking that, in my opinion, lessens their effectiveness. This is just my opinion, but in my two decades of training, I have seen the specter of political correctness (PC) invade the training world.

PC is a funny thing. It often starts as an understandable reaction to insensitivity and conditions that most reasonable people agree need to change. My training experience as a 10-year-old boy is just one example of the type of situation that untold numbers of people experienced and wanted to change. Thirty years ago, many training techniques were based on what is called "compulsion training." This means dogs were taught to respond in order to avoid punishment.

For example, a common method in those days to teach a dog not to jump up on people was to sharply say "No" and knee the dog in the chest. Almost no one was suggesting that clients physically injure their dogs, but clearly, training techniques based primarily on physical punishment run the risk of doing just that.

Additionally, some trainers really did take physical correction to very severe levels. Other "methods" from those days included such gems as stopping a dog from digging by filling the hole with water, taking the dog over to the hole and sticking the dog's head in the water-filled crater. Nipping—not aggression, but the common nibbling on fingers that puppies often engage in—was routinely addressed by "chucking the dog under the chin." This is a polite way of saying slapping the dog. Obviously, methods like these needed to change. And to a large degree, thanks in part to several new generations of trainers (myself included), they did. But then, because it's probably human nature, the pendulum began to swing in the opposite direction.

Nowadays, there are people who consider the use of *any* correction or punishment to be "cruel." Today, there are those who object to the use of terms like "problem solving" or "problem dogs." Their logic is: Who's to say what is or isn't a problem? They go on to say that most problem dog behaviors are only problematic for humans. Dogs naturally chew. Many naturally dig, bark and engage in numerous other doggie behaviors. It is arrogant for humans to arbitrarily decide that certain behaviors are unacceptable or bad. I have been told that any attempt to train and discipline a dog smacks of "species-ism!" That is, one species (humans) dominating another (canines). I swear, I'm not making this up. Some of these same people object to the use of the term "owner."

For example, I use the word "owner" in this book. I say things like "dog owners should remember" or a "good owner tries to understand why their dog does what it does." Fifteen years ago this wouldn't have even drawn a comment, but today there are people who object to the idea that one species should own another. There have been successful attempts in some communities to legally change the term "owner" to "guardian." People have suggested that ownership smacks of slavery, as though owning a dog is the same as one person owning another. In my mind there is a huge difference between owning a person, which neither I nor (I hope) anyone in this country supports, and owning a dog!

I think a word about definitions is in order here. Words have meaning, and over the last decade or so, the definitions of many words have been changing. I don't mean how they are defined in the *Oxford* or *Webster's Dictionary,* but about how everyday people use certain words. Often, those who control what words mean can control a debate.

When trainers are afraid to say things like "dog owner," when owners are confused after being told that any type of correction is cruel, when people spend months trying to modify their dog's behaviors using any method as long as no correction is involved (lest they be labeled "abusive"), when devices like slip collars, commonly called "choke chains," are labeled cruel under any circumstances and there is talk of outlawing them, I have to stand up and shout, "ENOUGH!"

Some people might be wondering why I'm even bringing this up. This is the main reason I wrote this book. Specifically, I wrote it to share many of the advances in training that have occurred in the last 30 years, while at the same time publicly stating that not everything trainers did 30 years ago, and for hundreds of years before that, was wrong, backwards or cruel; and to state that punishment exists in nature and has a place in training. I do this not to enhance my reputation among trainers, but to help owners (there's that word) effectively train their pets, so that both can enjoy better lives together.

So, now that you have a little background about me and why I wrote this book, I hope you're intrigued enough to read on!

I will begin by talking about when training should start (hint: right away), then move on to a chapter about how your dog learns. From there, we'll discuss the proper way to make your dog a comfortable member of your family. The focus will then shift to addressing common behavior problems, obedience and ways to screen and locate a professional trainer. For those of you who are interested, there is even a section on how to become a trainer, as well as a resource guide showing you where to find a ton of information about dogs on the Internet. I sincerely hope all of you find this book as rewarding to read as I found it to write. So let's get started. Let's get training.

CHAPTER 2

IF YOU HAVE A DOG, YOU ARE A TRAINER

Whenever I am out in public and speak with people, whether it's at a social gathering or just meeting someone, I often hear the question "What do you do for a living?" When I tell people my profession, it almost always sparks curiosity and genuine interest. Of course, as any dog trainer will tell you, it also stimulates about a trillion questions—which is why I sometimes cringe when I know the "what do you do" question is about to be asked. However, most of the time it is fun to talk about and a good topic of conversation.

One of the most common questions I hear is, "How old does my dog have to be to start training?" My answer has always been the same: "From the minute you get your dog home, you are training her. If you have a dog, you are a trainer." Often this response earns me confused looks. After all, most people have heard things like, "Wait until the dog is six months old before training" or, "Get your dog into puppy classes at twelve to sixteen weeks."

Thirty years ago, the six-month rule was fairly common. This was due, in part, to the fact that all too often training classes in those days involved strong physical corrections, and a puppy younger than six months might be physically or emotionally damaged if she was trained that way before the six-month mark. As you can well imagine, putting a 12-week-old puppy on a choke chain and administering sharp leash corrections was generally a very harsh way to train, and sometimes caused real problems.

Fortunately—and this is one of the good things that has happened in the last 10 to 12 years—training methods have become far gentler. It is also pretty much universally understood in the training community that a great deal of effective training can be accomplished with puppies at a very young age. We have many trainers to thank for this, including such visionaries as Dr. Ian Dunbar. Trainers like Dunbar and others, including the ones in my company, have tried to communicate the importance of formal training at a young age.

Formal training—that is, training with a professional instructor in group or private lessons, or even in a kennel—can and does start much earlier now than in the past. However, my "if you have a dog, you are a trainer" answer goes a bit deeper than that. What I would like owners to understand in this chapter is that any time you interact with your dog, you are teaching your dog something. All too often what happens is that owners inadvertently teach their dogs the wrong lessons, without realizing they're teaching lessons at all. This makes it tougher to train the dogs formally later on. Let's look at some examples.

WHAT ARE YOU TEACHING?

Mr. and Mrs. Jones are very excited about getting their 14-week-old Basset Hound puppy, and who wouldn't be? Alright, I'll admit it, I have a soft spot in my heart for Bassets. They're just so cute, and since I'm writing this book, the Joneses agree! So, Mr. and Mrs. Jones bring their 14-week-old Basset Hound puppy named Buford to their home. They put Buford on the living room floor and, like the true hound he is, Buford starts sniffing and wandering around. No harm there. Then Buford sees a table leg. This looks interesting and, after smelling it, Buford starts to lightly chew on it. He's doing what all puppies do:

investigating his environment using the physical tools he has at his disposal. In this regard he is no different from you, me or a two-year-old child. However, since Buford doesn't have hands, he will put things in his mouth a bit more frequently than you or I would.

When the Joneses see their puppy chewing the table, Mr. Jones tells Buford, "Hey, no, stop that." Buford, thoroughly engrossed in the world of oak, ignores Mr. Jones, and Mr. Jones, seeing this, repeats his "command." "Hey, Buford, no! Stop!" Buford continues to chew and Mr. Jones, a little bit frustrated, walks over and gently pushes Buford away from the table. Buford looks at Mr. Jones, walks three or four feet away, and then squats and pees. Both Mr. and Mrs. Jones yell "No!" pick Buford up and take him out in the backyard, where they put him down and in a stern voice say, "Bad dog, go out here, not inside."

Does any of this sound familiar? I've seen variations of this thousands of times. What owners don't realize is that a lot is being taught to the dog in this scenario. Please read it again, and this time, count the number of times the Joneses gave commands to their dog that the dog ignored. Of course, there is no reason this dog should have responded to the commands, since he wasn't born knowing what they mean. You and I know the command "no" means a dog should stop whatever he is doing, but in the scenario I've just described, "no" was given on at least two occasions when the dog chewed the table leg, with absolutely nothing else following it. At best, this teaches the dog not to listen to the word "no," especially if this scenario is repeated five or six times a day for a month or two—or three.

Additionally, and even more importantly, the Joneses have not yet learned the concepts of prevention and redirection. That is, they haven't learned how to teach Buford what to chew on, so that they can strongly praise correct chewing behavior as opposed to just reacting to what he shouldn't do. For example, when Buford was initially placed on the floor inside, there should have been proper chew toys available for his exploration. What's more, Buford should not have been placed on the floor in the house unless he had gone to the bathroom outside first, then been praised for it and given a little extra time outside to make sure he had eliminated completely.

Basically what the Joneses taught Buford was:

◆ Not to listen to "no."

◆ Table legs are available and interesting items to chew.

◆ If you have to pee, the living room is as good a spot as any.

◆ The backyard might not be a nice place, because this is where the large creatures take me and then yell.

Of course, Mr. and Mrs. Jones didn't mean to do any of this. They, like so many other owners, didn't realize that if they have a dog, they are training from the first second.

The above scenario won't really teach this dog all of these things after one single time, but many owners repeat this scenario, or scenes just like it, hundreds and hundreds of times—most prior to "formal" training.

OFF-LEASH CONTROL

Another challenge with young puppies involves obedience commands and raises a huge question regarding off-leash versus on-leash control. Basically it works like this.

Most people need and want their dog to respond to obedience commands when the dog is not wearing a leash. This is not to say that most owners want their dogs to walk down a busy street off leash. In fact, this can be dangerous no matter how well trained your dog is, and may also violate local leash laws. That being said, your dog doesn't live on a leash and, as such, has to listen to some commands off the leash. Which commands? The recall ("come") is critical, as is "stay," "sit" and probably "down."

Off-leash control needs to be attained, at the very least, around the house, in the yard and possibly in the neighborhood. The big question is, when does obedience training start and how does an owner typically go about getting off-leash control of this type?

The real answer is, obedience training starts from the very second *you,* the owner, start giving your dog obedience commands. Most owners start giving their dog commands on the very first day.

When should formal training start? The answer varies, because generally your dog will need to have some inoculations before being admitted to a class with other dogs. Speak to your veterinarian about this, but please understand that diseases such as parvovirus and distemper are nothing to ignore. They can be nasty, fatal and can strike puppies who are not inoculated against them. Typically most classes won't allow young puppies to be enrolled before 14 weeks of age. If you get your dog at 10 weeks of age, this means a month before you start any kind of formal training. It is during this month that most owners start to make mistakes that often make obedience training much more difficult to teach down the road.

Conventional training wisdom goes something like this: When you start formal training, you put the dog on a leash and some form of training collar. For many years the training collar most commonly used was a metal-link slip collar, usually called a choke chain. There are numerous choke chain variations. Some links are bigger, some smaller, some irregularly shaped, some are made of nylon, but all work on the

Choke chains.

same noose-type principle. That is, when you pull one end of the collar, it tightens around the dog's neck. When you release that end, the collar loosens again.

Prong collars, sometimes called pinch collars, were once also routinely used. These devices work in a similar fashion to a choke chain, but the prongs pinch the dog's neck when the collar tightens. It sounds worse than it is, but it is clearly not a device designed to be pleasurable for your dog.

A pinch collar.

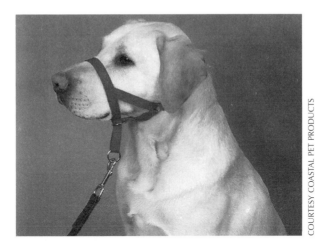

COURTESY COASTAL PET PRODUCTS

The Halti, an excellent head collar.

Nowadays—and I think this is a huge improvement—head collars that fit over the dog's head and muzzle are replacing choke chains as the collar of choice. It's an improvement (for most dogs) because these collars enable handlers to more easily control the dog's body with less force by controlling the dog's head. This is very similar to the way some horses are trained. For a number of years, there was a huge debate in the training world (trainers love to debate) about whether head collars or choke chains worked better and whether choke chains were cruel or inhumane. I believed then, as I do now, that both collars are effective and, when used properly, neither is inhumane. Personally, I believe head harnesses are better in most, but not all, training situations.

So, as I started to say, conventional training wisdom has you in class with your dog on a leash and some type of training collar. The objective is to train the dog to listen well enough on the leash that he can be consistently counted on to obey all commands regardless of distractions. When this occurs (and in the best case it can take four to six months), the hope is that you will be able to take the leash off and the dog will still obey you on the first command off leash, initially with no distractions and eventually with them. It makes sense—unless you've ever tried it. If you have, then you know what typically happens.

COURTESY PREMIER PET PRODUCTS

The Gentle Leader, another
excellent head collar.

When you take the leash off, the dog is far less inclined to listen. In some instances, the dog doesn't listen at all! I've seen dogs who were absolutely, perfectly obedient on leash completely "forget" their training when the leash came off.

Entire training methods have been developed to overcome this problem. These include light lines, where a very light nylon cord or even monofilament is put on the dog's collar, so that when the leash is taken off the handler can step on the monofilament or grab it (with gloves), thus preventing the dog from escaping and teaching him that you still have control.

Smaller leashes, or gradually cutting a six-foot leash to five feet, four feet, two feet, etc., have also been used. This is because we've all seen dogs who listen perfectly on a six-foot leash. You could even drop the six-foot leash and walk 10, 20 or 40 feet away and the dog would still listen. If a dog listens on a six-foot leash when you're 40 feet away, is the leash really necessary? Many people would say no and remove the leash. The problem is, when you take the leash off, the dog often runs away. To overcome this, instead of taking the leash off you start to gradually cut it down. First five feet, then four, until finally the dog is left wearing the metal clip portion of the leash. Many dogs responded to this technique, although some started to run when the leash got shorter than one or two feet. Many trainers still find the challenge of getting dogs to listen off leash among the most difficult they have to deal with.

To be fair, this is less of a problem now than it was 30 years ago. There are several reasons for this, including the fact that most modern training methods are not based on teaching your dog to avoid leash corrections. When compulsion methods of this type were taught, the dog viewed the leash as the tool of correction. The problem was that once the tool was removed, the threat of correction and the ability to correct were also removed. Dogs are not stupid. If they're trained to avoid punishment, and the instrument of punishment is gone, so is the dog— down the street, with his handler chasing 100 feet behind.

The other reason this is less of a problem today is that training usually starts at a younger age now than it did in decades past. When owners waited until their dogs were six to eight months old before they started formal training, they had been interacting with their pets for months before formal training took place. During this time, they were inadvertently teaching their dogs not to listen. To put it another way, if you only have a month to mess up your dog's training, you will typically do less damage than if you have five months.

I can just hear owners asking me, "Wait a minute. What do I do that teaches my dog not to listen to me?" The bad news is, *plenty.* The good news is, it can all be avoided. Let's look at another scenario.

Going back to the Jones' house, we see them and their 14-week-old Basset Hound puppy. The puppy, named Buford, is in the bedroom doing what Bassets do best, sniffing. Suddenly Buford's keen nose smells something incredibly exciting, an old sock under a dresser. He smells it and, intrigued, tastes it. Yummy, salty, interesting, this warrants further investigation. He takes it in his mouth and starts to walk around the room. Mrs. Jones sees this and says to Buford, "Buford, honey, don't chew that. Come. Come to mommy." Buford ignores this and starts to walk out of the room carrying the sock. Mrs. Jones follows saying, "No Buford, come. Come. Come. Come here right now." This has absolutely no effect and Mrs. Jones moves quickly toward the dog in an attempt to grab the inappropriate object out of Buford's mouth. Upon seeing what, from the dog's perspective, is a large creature moving toward him, Buford reacts instinctively by darting away. Fourteen-week-old Basset puppies are not exactly renowned for their speed, but they can be wicked around corners, and Buford manages to get halfway across the house before dropping the sock. He continues to run and is successful in avoiding capture. Mrs. Jones stopped chasing him after he dropped the sock anyway, but Buford doesn't understand any of that. He simply knows he ran and got away. Mrs. Jones picks up the sock and thinks to herself, "Gosh, this is going to be work. But I guess he learned I don't want him to chew socks."

Actually, it is extremely unlikely that the Jones' dog learned anything like not to chew socks from the above scenario. What the dog did learn (or will learn if this scenario is repeated) are a number of things, none of them good.

First, the command "come" was given six times and the dog not only didn't come, but ultimately ran the other way. Let's look at this for a second. This interaction took place off leash. This type of interaction could reoccur 10 times a day for a month or longer. This means Buford would hear the "come" command 60 times every day and never listen. Sixty times a day for a month is roughly 1,800 times that Buford learned not to come! Is it any surprise that after 1,800 repetitions of not listening to the "come" command off leash, when Buford is taken to class, given the "come" command on leash and then consistently taught to obey it on the leash, that he will only learn to respond to "come" on leash? He's already learned not to come off leash. This is the crux of the problem.

Second, Buford also learned that running away was successful. Not a very good lesson for any dog to learn.

BASIC TRAINING PRINCIPLES

So what can owners do about this? A number of things. First, continue to read this book, because many of the principles and methods found here can be started from day one. As you read, you will learn how to prevent problems and how to redirect, focus and reward your dog for correct behavior, rather than just react, yell and give ineffective commands when you're confronted with unacceptable behavior. Hopefully, you will also learn the crucial principles of training, so you can teach your dog what I call "foundation level" off-leash training, and, very importantly, teach this type of training whenever possible before you start on-leash work. Will this be easier to teach if you've just obtained a puppy? Yes, but dogs of any age can benefit from these training principles.

Here are some basic principles that all dog owners need to learn and follow:

1. **Be consistent.** A behavior is either acceptable or it isn't. It can't be acceptable on alternate Tuesdays when you're in the mood. For example, it can't be OK to allow your dog to jump all over you on the weekends when you're in casual clothes, but not during the week when you're dressed for work. That's an obvious one, although you'd be amazed how many people I've met who do exactly that.

   Here's one that's less obvious. It can't be OK for your dog to chew fabric toys but not to chew "inappropriate" fabric items. In other words, if you give your dog an old sock and say, "Here, chew this," don't be surprised when she eats your shirt.

   Consistency is a bit easier for singles or couples, and toughest for families. The more people who interact with the dog, the greater the likelihood of inconsistency. I strongly recommend that families conduct a few meetings to discuss and agree upon what will be universally unacceptable behavior on the part of the dog. Everyone needs to clearly understand what the rules will be for a training program to be most successful. That being said, we live in the real world and I recognize how difficult consistency on the part of a six-year-old child will likely be. Parents of younger children will need to practice a fair amount of prevention and understand that the dog's training process may be a little bit more difficult and prolonged.

2. **Be consistent.** Yes, I know I already said this, but consistency also extends to obedience commands. If you want your dog to learn to listen to obedience commands the first time they're given, you need to be prepared to properly teach your dog to obey them the first time. This is most effectively accomplished if the initial foundation-level obedience you teach around the house is done off leash.

   I have sometimes run into problems when discussing how important it is for dogs to obey commands consistently. In my opinion, this is an area where attitudes have gone downhill in the last 30 years. Decades ago the idea that a dog needed to obey commands the first time they were given would not have drawn comment. Today, there are many owners who are uncomfortable with the idea that their dog should be trained to respond so predictably. I've had owners object, based on the idea that they did not want their dogs "to become robots." It is important for these owners to understand that, first of all, if training is primarily done with compassion and reward this will not happen; and second of all, you might not care if your dog listens on the first command until the very first time she runs out into the street. Then, as cars are barreling toward her, you will pray she listens on the first command, because you may never get a second one.

   The specifics of how to teach foundation-level obedience off leash can be found in Chapter 7 of this book. However, the principles of consistency really need to be understood here.

3. **Understand why behaviors take place and deal with problems by dealing with the cause.** When owners learn to do this, they will not just be reacting to what are often symptoms of an underlying problem.

4. **Learn basic training techniques and then follow rules one and two.** All owners need to understand the principles of prevention, maintenance, redirection, reward and correction. And they need to use them consistently.

Now that you have an understanding of some of the challenges, let's discuss a little bit about behavior, so that everyone can be clear what terms such as "prevention," "maintenance," "redirection" and "reward" really mean. Once you understand how a dog learns, we can get on to the business of training. Please proceed to Chapter 3!

How Your Dog Learns: A Basic Primer That Makes Sense, Without a Lot of Jargon and Psychobabble

This chapter will help you understand the scientific principles of how dogs learn. Since all learning is governed by these basic principles, learning them can help you develop better training skills through a proper understanding of behavior.

Over the last 15 years, it has become increasingly difficult for owners to translate the behavioral jargon used by some dog trainers. This is made even more difficult by the fact that trainers sometimes misuse behavioral terms. In addition, although most people today are somewhat familiar with behavioral terms, they are often confused about what these terms really mean. For example, what do "positive reinforcement," "positive training," "punishment" and "negative reinforcement" really mean? It is important for owners to have a basic understanding of these terms and others, and how they apply to your dog's training.

Part of what causes confusion is that no single training method works in every situation. The reason for this is that every dog, environment and owner is unique. With an unlimited number of possible scenarios, it stands to reason that there will be more than one way to modify and/or teach various behaviors to dogs and owners. This is part of the reason why five trainers can have five different ideas about how to teach the same thing. A famous trainer and author once said that if you put 10 trainers in a room and ask them their opinion about something, the only thing they'll agree on is that the other nine don't know what they're talking about. This makes it challenging for dog owners, to say the least.

Owners who understand basic behavioral principles will find it easier to make training decisions based on facts. This is important, because when trainers use unproven or unscientific methods, the results may not be good. It may even be counterproductive. As such, it is crucial that training techniques be rooted in science.

Please read this chapter twice. The first time, try to read it straight through. Then read it a second time, pausing to consider the different examples and concepts I cover. It's my experience that this will help you "get it." Let's start with some basic terms: motivation, reinforcement and punishment.

MOTIVATION

Motivation is a need, drive or desire that incites a person or animal to some action or behavior. All learning entails some change in behavior. In order to change, the dog must be *motivated* to change. If there is no motivation, no change or learning will occur.

There are two main types of motivation: positive and negative. With *positive motivation,* the dog works to get things *the dog* likes. Examples of positive motivation include:

◆ Walks

◆ Attention

- Petting
- Rubs
- Playing with other dogs
- Food treats
- Playing with toys
- Getting to sniff
- Car rides
- Going outside
- Access to a favorite resting place
- Scratches

Here's an example of how positive motivation is used in training: Shred, a six-month-old American Eskimo Dog, runs to her owner and sits when she first greets him. Shred is petted and scratched for sitting. This is something Shred likes. Shred is positively motivated to sit for pets and scratches.

Negative motivation is when the dog works to avoid something *the dog* considers unpleasant. Examples of negative motivation include:

- A spray of water
- Choke chain corrections
- Not getting a food treat
- Raising your voice
- A shock from an electronic shock collar or mat
- Loud noise from a motion sensor alarm
- Citronella spray
- Being ignored
- Losing her toys
- Losing her playmate

Here's an example of how negative motivation is used in training: Sometimes Shred gets so excited that she jumps on her owner when greeting him. The owner responds by turning away and ignoring her. Shred considers this unpleasant and she is negatively motivated to not jump, so she can avoid being ignored.

You can use both positive motivation and negative motivation to either reinforce/increase a behavior or punish/reduce/eliminate a behavior.

Reinforcement

Reinforcement means to give new strength or force to a behavior; for training purposes, it means to do something to strengthen a behavior. If you want to increase the probability that a certain response will occur, some sort of reinforcement must be involved. This may include negative reinforcement or positive reinforcement.

Reinforcement must be something meaningful enough for the dog to try to get (positive reinforcement) or try to avoid (negative reinforcement). And it must be meaningful *to the dog*.

TRAINING EXAMPLE	
Desired behavior	Shred needs to learn to stay off the couch.
Positive reinforcement	Positively reinforce Shred for staying off the couch by feeding her food treats when she's on the floor in her safe spot.
Negative reinforcement	Negatively reinforce Shred for staying off the couch by giving relief from the loud noise of a motion sensitive sound alarm, which stops making noise the instant she jumps off the couch.

The box on page 28 demonstrates how either negative or positive reinforcement can be used to obtain a desired behavior. Look at the box carefully, because that last part on negative reinforcement can cause some confusion. The negative reinforcement does not take place when the noise starts, but rather when the noise stops.

Since trainers use terms like *positive reinforcment* and *negative reinforcement* all the time, let's review to make sure you are very clear about what these terms mean.

Positive reinforcement involves *giving* reinforcement at the moment the dog performs the desirable behavior, to increase the likelihood the dog will perform that behavior again. An example is giving your dog a food treat the moment she achieves the sitting position.

Negative reinforcement involves *removing* something the dog considers unpleasant the instant she performs the desired behavior. An example is releasing the pressure on a flat buckle collar the moment the dog achieves the sitting position.

Training methods can contain both positive and negative reinforcement.

Punishment

Nowhere is the controversy greater in dog training than on the subject of punishment. There are many reasons for this, including a backlash from the many years punishment was very commonly used as a primary way of training dogs. For most people, it is also far less pleasurable to think in terms of punishment than it is to think about praise or reward. After all, wouldn't it be great if all you need is love? My answer, like that of almost everyone, is "Yes!" However, while it surely would be great, that's not how the real world works. In the real world, punishment has a place in training. Not a primary place, but a place nonetheless. So what does punishment mean? Is punishment cruel?

First, *punishment* can be defined as a penalty imposed or any ill suffered as a consequence of wrongdoing.

Sounds kind of ominous, doesn't it? It is here that the debate begins. Is punishment cruel? It depends on what the punishment is. For example, if Shred jumps up on her owner and her owner responds by striking Shred with a stick the instant Shred jumps, I would say without question this punishment is cruel. Why? Because such a reaction runs a very real risk of physically harming Shred. What's more, because this punishment is likely to be very painful, a whole host of other problems may manifest themselves as a result. For instance, Shred might become afraid any time her owner holds a similar object. This fear might become generalized to all people holding objects. Shred might, in her fear, become aggressive. Shred might be injured. Obviously, no knowledgeable, enlightened trainer would recommend such a method. If any of you encounter a trainer who does, steer clear of that trainer.

The question is, just because the example above illustrates that some punishment can indeed be cruel, does that mean all punishment is cruel? My answer is, "Absolutely not." It depends on the punishment. As a general rule, punishment needs to be associated with the behavior, not the person or persons administering it. Additionally, and very importantly, punishment must not cause physical or emotional harm to your pet.

When a punishing stimulus is a consequence of a certain behavior, it will decrease the likelihood of that particular behavior occurring again. The punishment must be something the dog feels is either unpleasant enough to avoid experiencing (positive punishment) or valuable enough to avoid losing (negative punishment).

The kind of *positive punishment* where you say "no, no, no" to the dog and wag your finger may not be unpleasant enough for the dog to really want to avoid. However, she may try to avoid a choke chain correction. This is an important point. Some people are so uncomfortable with the idea of punishment, they have a tendency to use extremely mild levels. Unfortunately this can often be ineffective. You need to find a balance—the mildest correction possible that still has meaning for your dog.

Trying to *negatively punish* a dog by withholding petting will not work if the dog doesn't care that much about being petted. However, withholding a ball the dog loves to play with would negatively punish some behaviors. This is another important point, and involves knowing your dog well enough to understand what really motivates her.

TRAINING EXAMPLE

Undesired behavior	Shred is jumping all over you.
Positive punishment	Use a tug on the leash to get Shred off you when she jumps on you.
Negative punishment	Turn your back on Shred, ignoring her completely for two or three seconds, thus depriving Shred of your attention when she jumps on you.

So to review:

Positive punishment involves *presenting* a negative consequence to an undesirable behavior the moment the dog engages in the undesirable behavior. It is here where a professional trainer can really make a difference. Punishment the instant an undesirable behavior takes place requires practice and timing—timing that often separates a professional trainer from a layperson. Punishment *after* a behavior has taken place will be ineffective and counterproductive in training.

An example of proper positive punishment: saying "No!" the instant your dog chews on the couch.

An example of improper (and ineffective) positive punishment: coming home, seeing your dog has chewed on the couch, taking the dog over to the couch and telling the dog "No!"

Negative punishment involves *removing* something good from the dog at the moment the dog performs an undesirable behavior.

An example of proper negative punishment: taking away the dog's free, supervised access in your den the instant she starts chewing on your couch.

An example of improper (and ineffective) negative punishment: Coming home, seeing your dog has chewed on the couch and then ignoring the dog for the rest of the evening to punish her for chewing on your couch. (She won't get it!)

Now that we've covered some of the basics, let's get a little more complex.

BEHAVIOR CONDITIONING

There are two primary behavior conditioning styles—*classical conditioning* and *operant conditioning*—both of which are useful in shaping behavior.

Shaping means reinforcing the dog for a portion of the correct response and gradually asking for more and more until the dog has learned the entire behavior. For example, when you call your dog to you, at first you might praise her the instant she turns and starts in your direction. After several days of this, you might only start to praise her as she gets closer to you. Eventually, she might only receive praise for coming all the way to you.

Classical Conditioning

Classical conditioning is also sometimes called Pavlovian conditioning. This is best defined as the dog *understanding* a simple association.

For many dog owners, the name Pavlov no doubt rings a bell. Ivan Pavlov was not a dog trainer. In fact, his main interest was digestion. From 1891 through 1900, Pavlov studied the digestive process in dogs, particularly salivation and its role in assisting digestion. As he conducted his studies, Pavlov realized that without salivation, the stomach didn't receive the message to start digesting food. Pavlov then attempted to see if he could start salivation without the stimulus of food. To do this, he rang a bell whenever he gave the dogs something to eat. Eventually, he stopped giving them the food and just rang the bell. When he did, his dogs would begin to salivate even though there was no food present. Pavlov published these results in 1903, calling the response a *conditioned reflex,* and distinguishing it from an innate or involuntary reflex such as pulling one's hand away from a hot stove.

This process by which his dogs learned to associate the sound of the bell with the food was dubbed *conditioning*.

Operant Conditioning

This is best defined as having a dog understand that a particular behavior the dog *chooses* to do has a particular consequence. Let's say you want to teach a dog to back away from a piece of food whenever you ring a bell. To understand how operant conditioning works, follow the steps below:

Bell → dog backs away from food → dog gets food

Bell → dog moves toward food → dog doesn't get food

With operant conditioning, there is always a consequence to every behavior. In the above example, the dog must *learn* to back away from the food at the sound of the bell in order to get the food. Backing away

---

THE OPPOSITION REFLEX

Compulsion trainers, that is, trainers who physically force dogs to engage in certain behaviors, sometimes have a problem teaching behaviors that are opposite of the reflexive response dogs normally have. This is caused, in part, by the *opposition reflex*. People have an opposition reflex too. Anyone who has experienced someone pushing on their chest in an attempt to get them to move probably remembers an instinctive reaction of resistance. You probably pushed forward against the force pushing you backward. The force of the reaction is different with different people, and runs the gamut from mild resistance to extremely strong resistance. This is every bit as true in dogs.

The strength of the opposition reflex response dogs have to force depends on the dog and the amount of force used. Typical reactions are for dogs to crunch up their bodies, freeze, lie down and/or move away. Anyone attempting to force their dog to sit may have experienced their dog resisting the force or crunching up and lying down as a response to the force.

Trainers who depend on using force can sometimes find themselves in a vicious training cycle when the technique they are trying to use actually prompts the dog to engage in the opposite behavior.

---

from the food is not an automatic or natural response to food (as is salivating or moving toward food), but rather something the dog must *learn* to do. This is what distinguishes it as operant conditioning.

Continuing on our behavioral journey of understanding, it is important to next learn a bit more about reinforcement.

REINFORCEMENT

There are two types of reinforcement:

1. Unconditioned reinforcement (primary reinforcement)
2. Conditioned reinforcement (secondary reinforcement)

Unconditioned reinforcement, also known as primary reinforcement, is something that is essential for the dog's survival or something the dog really likes. Because these are natural things such as food, air and water, the dog doesn't have to be taught (or conditioned) that these are rewarding.

Examples of unconditioned reinforcers include:

◆ Food

◆ Water

◆ Air

◆ Shelter

◆ Toys

◆ Praise and petting

Toys, praise and petting are often considered conditioned reinforcers, but a dog with high play drive and a lot of energy or an especially sensitive dog may consider them an unconditioned reinforcer. For example, a Labrador Retriever who instinctively loves to fetch will naturally consider toys she can retrieve to be unconditioned reinforcers. *The dog determines what her unconditioned reinforcers are, not the owner or the trainer.*

Not all unconditioned reinforcers have the same value. Some dogs like food more than toys, and others like toys more than food. Most people also consider praise and petting to be an unconditioned reinforcer for dogs, but not all dogs like praise and petting. This is why it's important for owners to know their dogs. It is also why trainers need to be open-minded and flexible. For example, some trainers use food in all their training. The problem is that not all dogs are motivated by food. If a trainer isn't flexible enough to modify or change methods based on individual dogs' personalities and preferences, you need to find a better trainer.

Conditioned reinforcement, also known as secondary reinforcement, is something that has no inherent meaning to the dog, but the dog *learns* to consider positive. In other words, the dog has to *learn* that a conditioned reinforcer is good. Dogs learn some conditioned reinforcers on their own, as they live with us.

Examples of conditioned reinforcers include:

◆ Going for a walk

◆ Putting on the leash (this can indicate going for a walk)

◆ Sound of a can opener (indicates food is coming)

◆ Praise and petting from people

◆ Doorbell (can indicate that people are coming to play)

◆ Toys

◆ The word "good" or "yes"

◆ The sound of a clicker

We want to teach the dog to associate positive things with certain verbal commands. Typically, we use the word "good" or "yes," or the sound of a clicker. (A clicker is a small plastic device that, when depressed by your finger or thumb, makes an audible clicking noise. Some trainers find clickers to be more effective than verbal commands.) These conditioned reinforcers signal, "You just did the right thing and are about to receive a reward for it!"

Important Points to Remember About Reinforcers

1. Understanding how conditioned and unconditioned reinforcement works is crucial for good dog training. These principles are used when teaching a dog obedience commands using positive reinforcement. Developing strong conditioned reinforcers strengthens the communication between dog and owner, which leads to happier, more energetic obedience and a closer relationship between you and your dog.

2. The first thing to teach your dog is one verbal (command) or audible (clicker) conditioned reinforcer. This conditioned reinforcer will enable you to communicate to the dog that she did something correct and will be rewarded for it. Learning a conditioned reinforcer will help the dog make a strong positive association between the reinforcer and various rewards. Once this is accomplished, the word (or click) and the rewards will become interchangeable for the dog. This will enable you to communicate correct behavior to your dog by simply saying "good" or "yes" or clicking the instant a correct behavior takes place.

3. Remember, Pavlov taught us that dogs learn by association. When there is a *predictable* relationship between two events, the dog learns to respond to the first event in *anticipation* of the second event.

   Here's an example: Every single time your dog hears the doorbell ring, the door is opened and there is a person to sniff and jump on. The dog gets excited when the doorbell rings because it means guaranteed sniffs and greetings. The doorbell is never rung without that sound being followed by the excitement of greeting a person.

   Here is another example: Every single time you say "good," you immediately follow up by giving your dog a food treat. This teaches your dog to connect the first event (the word "good") with the second event (a food treat). If you do this many times, your dog will start to anticipate food treats upon hearing the word "good."

Some of you may find this topic fascinating. Others may find it tough going. I encourage everyone to keep reading, because it's important.

THE STAGES OF LEARNING

In my 20-plus years of training, I have found that there are four stages of learning:

1. Acquisition

2. Automation

3. Generalization

4. Maintenance

Stage 1: Acquisition

During the acquisition stage of training, the dog learns through shaping and reinforcement that a specific new behavior is rewarding. She will then choose to engage in that behavior again and again so she can continue to receive the rewards she likes

For example, the dog is introduced to the "sit" command by being silently lured with food into the sit position. To do this, you hide a small piece of food in your fist, bring it in front of the dog's nose and then slowly over the dog's muzzle and top of her head. Your hand is usually no more than three to four inches from the dog. Most dogs will lift their heads up to follow your hand and sit as your hand moves backwards over their head and out of their sight. Once the dog is in the sitting position, you say "sit" once. Then you immediately mark or signal to the dog that this sit behavior was good by saying "good" and popping a treat into the dog's mouth for completing the sit. If you do this correctly, your dog will learn to associate the command "sit" with the behavior of sitting. Also, and very critically, the dog will learn that sitting is a behavior that is rewarding for her to engage in.

Criteria for moving to the next stage of training

When the dog learns to anticipate the action (that is, she sits) *before* you can complete the food-lure motion, you are ready to move to the automation stage of training.

The dog should anticipate the action approximately 90 percent of the time before moving to the next stage of training.

Stage 2: Automation

The dog learns to automatically offer a specific behavior to a particular command without being lured.

Example: You say "sit" once and the dog sits without any food-luring movements from your hands. In this stage, the dog is initially rewarded all the time (known as a continuous reinforcement schedule). This means the word "good" is always followed by food. Later the dog can be put on a variable reinforcement schedule (the word "good" is followed by food only for the better sits).

An automatic response is when the dog moves into the sit position each time you say "sit."

Criteria for moving to the next stage of training

You are ready to move to the generalization stage of training when your dog responds correctly to the command approximately 90 percent of the time in a familiar environment.

For example, your dog automatically sits when you say "sit" in the corner of your living room, where you have been practicing with the dog.

Stage 3: Generalization

The dog learns that even if different people give the command in different locations and in slightly different ways, the response should be the same.

For example, the dog has at least a 90 percent compliance rate for "sit" in the living room, with the original person who trained her standing right in front of the dog while giving the command. To begin teaching the dog to generalize the behavior, start changing one aspect of the situation at a time. For instance, the person training the dog can continue training in the living room but stand slightly sideways or away from the dog. Eventually, they can give the "sit" command when they are sitting in a chair or standing across the room.

Different people can train the dog, starting in the living room. They should give the dog the "sit" command when they are standing right in front of the dog. Once the dog masters this, they, too, can stand sideways or away from the dog. They can eventually say the "sit" command while they are seated in a chair or standing across the room.

Continue this generalization process of changing various aspects of the "sit" command over several weeks. The dog will come to understand that she must sit in any situation when she is given the "sit" command.

Criteria for moving to the next stage of training

When the dog can correctly perform a command 90 percent of the time in various situations, with various distractions, she is ready to enter the maintenance stage of training.

Stage 4: Maintenance

When the dog is consistently complying with the command in a variety of situations 90 to 100 percent of the time, she is considered to be in the maintenance stage of training. Once the dog has achieved maintenance, you can feel comfortable that the dog has a complete understanding of the command. The amount of time it takes to reach this stage varies according to the dog, the owner and the complexity of the behavior or command being taught.

To maintain any behavior or command at any stage of training, you may need to go back a level if the dog makes mistakes. Going back a level means practicing the command the dog just disobeyed, but at an easier level. This will enable you to reinforce the proper response to the command before it deteriorates any further. A general rule is that one mistake requires going back a level for three to 10 repetitions.

For example, your dog has been doing perfect sit-stays for the past few weeks, even when guests come in the front door, until a friend comes in carrying their small dog. Upon seeing the small dog, your dog breaks her sit-stay and jumps up on the person. Just correcting the dog at that moment is not sufficient training. You should also go back a level by putting your dog in a sit-stay. Then have your friend walk out the front door and come in again without their dog. Once your dog is successful for three to 10 repetitions this way, try it again with the distraction of your friend holding their dog. Assuming your dog is successful at this point, have your dog do three to 10 sit-stays with the distraction of your friend holding their dog. Try asking this friend and other friends to help you set up this type of distraction a few times a week until you have a 90 to 100 percent response rate.

You can make the exercise easier by keeping your dog on leash and having the friend move slowly while holding their dog. This allows your dog to be successful so that you can reward a correct sit-stay again.

Hopefully, most of you are starting to see how the basic principles of behavior can be used to teach your dog. Now let's discuss corrections.

IMPORTANT POINTS TO REMEMBER ABOUT CORRECTIONS

1. If a physical correction is administered during the acquisition phase of a particular command, it may decrease the dog's desire to perform the command at all. This is sometime called *avoidance behavior.* It is important to build the dog's desire to perform a command. If you don't, and start administering corrections, you risk the dog trying to avoid the command. **This is why I don't like to give physical corrections until the dog clearly understands and obeys specific commands.** Then, assuming the dog "gets it" and chooses not to obey, corrections can be applied

effectively. This is very different from using corrections to try to teach new behavior.

A good example of the kinds of problems you run into if you use corrections too soon can be illustrated by the "down" command. If a dog's first introduction to "down" is to be forced by pulling the leash down or being pushed down at the shoulder blades, the dog may try to circumvent the entire process by moving away or resisting being pushed down. Remember the opposition reflex.

Instead, the owner should first use food luring to increase the dog's desire to lie down. Toy rewards can also be used. Regardless, the reward should be given to the dog the instant the dog is in the down position. This will encourage the dog to get down as quickly as possible to get the reward. **I would avoid corrections until at least the end of the automation stage.**

2. Corrections should be used sparingly. Because of this, training situations should be set up so that the dog will be receiving corrections no more frequently than 1 out of 10 commands. Remember, even a properly administered correction can make a response to a command worse, if the owner is grinding on the same exercise over and over. **Focus on success and rewarding it, as opposed to correction.** This means if the dog is being asked to perform a more difficult exercise and she makes a mistake after you give a correction, do not repeat the exercise in the same way that caused the dog to fail. This is why you typically go back a level, so you can reward proper behavior.

3. While corrections should be given sparingly, it is also critical that the correction be strong enough and occur at the right moment to extinguish the incorrect behavior in one or two attempts. I mentioned this earlier, but it's worth repeating.

4. The timing of the correction must be very specific. Slight changes in timing can have dramatic effects on learning. For example, if you are working with a dog on a long leash to develop a dependable recall ("come" command), the timing of the correction and

what you do after it will dictate what the dog learns. If you give the "come" command and correct the dog too early, not giving her sufficient time to respond, she may become uncomfortable leaving your side. If you correct her after she's turned toward you or for not coming fast enough, she may learn that coming is not a rewarding behavior. This is why it is so important for your dog to understand what you want before you use corrections.

Finally, let's discuss how dogs typically respond to stimuli.

RESPONSES TO STIMULI

There are eight types of responses to stimuli:

1. Single event learning
2. Orienting reflex
3. Desensitization
4. Sensitization
5. Adaptation/flooding
6. Learned irrelevance
7. Back-chaining
8. Pattern training

Single Event Learning

The dog judges every event that occurs in her life as either relevant or irrelevant.

Here's one example: A skateboard rolling down the sidewalk startles your dog and she yelps. You scream, run over to the dog and pick her up. You then carry her into the house and spend the rest of the afternoon soothing and caressing her on the sofa. The dog judges this event as *relevant*.

POSITIVE AND NEGATIVE CORRECTION

The word *correction* is used throughout this text. My use of the word refers to both positive punishment (adding something unpleasant) and negative punishment (taking away something pleasant). When choosing the type of correction to use, you should take into consideration the difficulty of the exercise and the temperament, drives and sensitivities of the dog. No single correction is right for every dog, and not all corrections involve physical force (that is, positive punishment).

Here is a partial list of positive punishers and negative punishers that are used in this book.

◆ Ignoring the dog

◆ Leash and collar correction

◆ Removing a treat or toy

◆ Sound correction or Scat Mat electric shock

Another example: You drop a glass in the kitchen sink and cut yourself. Your dog is startled by the noise, but since you are unaware that your dog is in the kitchen behind you and you are busy tending to your own cut finger, you don't rush to console the dog. Later you interact with the dog as though nothing happened, because you didn't see her being startled. The dog judges this event as *irrelevant*.

Taken together, skateboards are now extremely *relevant* to the dog and she is terrified of them, but the sound of breaking glass is *irrelevant*.

Orienting Reflex

Anything the dog perceives activates the orienting reflex. The orienting reflex may be used to redirect the dog's behavior. *This can be a very important training point.*

Here's one example: Your dog hears a clicker and reflexively turns her head in the direction the click is coming from.

Another example: Your dog barks at the window when people walk down the sidewalk. If you move away from the window and click the clicker, the dog should momentarily notice the click. You may then encourage the dog to move toward you and receive a treat.

You have redirected her behavior so she is being rewarded for changing her reaction to people walking down the sidewalk.

Over time, the dog will reflexively orient to *you* to receive treats and praise when she notices people on the sidewalk. The barking will lessen as the dog moves more quickly over to you to get her reward each time she sees people on the sidewalk. People on the sidewalk now have new meaning, and turning away from people on the sidewalk to receive a treat is more rewarding than barking at them.

Desensitization

This is also known as *habituation*. The dog learns to ignore a previously meaningful stimulus or unconditioned reflex (such as being startled by a loud noise).

Here's an example: A dog who has been struck in the face by a child must learn that every approach by a child does not mean she will be struck in the face. This is accomplished by controlling the dog's frame of mind when children approach during the retraining sessions. If the dog is put into a relaxed frame of mind with food treats, and is never allowed to become fearful or stressed during these approaches, the dog is much more likely to achieve desensitization.

Sensitization

This is the opposite of desensitization. It involves the dog becoming more sensitive to something.

Here's an example: A puppy gets taken to her first group class and, despite her nervousness and uncertainty about other dogs, her owner forces her to walk between two large adult dogs. At the next group class, the owner notices that the puppy doesn't even want to get out of the car. They again force the puppy to participate in the class. Because the owner forced the puppy into an overwhelming situation, instead of gradually allowing the puppy to participate in the class at her own speed, the puppy now shows more fear at each class.

Adaptation/Flooding

This involves exposing the dog to a stimulus to which she has been sensitized; the exposure is done to the point where the dog is too exhausted to respond to the presentation of the stimulus.

Here's an example: Your dog hates to be brushed. You might sit down and brush her until she stops reacting to the brushing—flooding her with the stimulus until she adapts. The point of this exercise is to prove to the dog that being brushed isn't so bad after all, and that the person brushing is not going to react to any of the dog's aggressive behaviors by stopping the brushing.

It is important to make sure that the brushing is not unpleasant in anyway. The dog must be brushed in a way that will not harm her, and precautions must be taken to prevent the dog from escaping or biting the person brushing her. The dog should be leashed to make escape impossible, and the person is protected from being bitten by wearing heavy gloves. The dog must realize that aggression will not get the person to stop brushing.

Note: *This method is extremely stressful to the dog.* You must not end the exercise (in this case the brushing) before the dog has achieved adaptation.

Learned Irrelevance

The dog ceases to pay attention to a particular stimulus (or command) because she has learned that it is of no consequence to her.

Here's an example: The dog no longer responds to "come" because the owner says "come" frequently when they have no way to get the dog to actually come. Therefore, the dog learns that "come" doesn't mean anything, so she ignores it.

Another example: The dog gets frantic each time you pick up the leash, because you *always* take her for a walk if you pick up the leash. If you start to pick up the leash 30 times a day and not take her for walk, the dog will come to ignore the leash because it means *nothing* to her.

Back-chaining

This means teaching the last behavior in a sequence first, then adding the other behaviors in reverse order until the dog learns a complete behavior sequence.

Here's an example: When the doorbell rings, you want the dog to go to the front door and sit on a mat while the door is opened and guests are invited in. Then you want the dog to push the door closed and come into the living room and lie on a mat. The first behavior you would teach is a down-stay on the mat. Then you would add going over to the mat. Then you would teach the dog to shut the door and then go over to the mat to lie down. Each time you add a behavior, you will have to give the dog rewards at the *end* of the new behavior, until the dog gets it. Then you make her go from the new behavior (shutting the door) to lying on the mat with no reward coming until she's on the mat. This will encourage her to go all the way to the last behavior to get her treat.

Continue to add behaviors until you have taught her to run to the mat at the door to sit—the first part of the chain. When you reach this point, the dog no longer gets any rewards during this series of behaviors. She must run through them all the way to the end before getting rewarded when she lies on the mat.

Can you figure out how to teach a retrieve using back-chaining?

Pattern Training

This is also known as *real life training*. It means finding out what patterns or routines exist in your daily schedule and fitting obedience training into that.

For example: Many people would like their dog to sit at the front door, come in and lie down near them in the living room, and come when they call the dog into the house from the back or front yard.

Therefore, you should focus on teaching "sit-stay" at the front door, "down-stay" in one location in the living room, and "come" from the back and front yard when you are standing in the doorway.

It is easier for the dog to learn obedience in these daily patterns than obedience in random locations. Teach your obedience where it counts most, first.

USING CONDITIONED REINFORCERS

It is crucial to understand that dogs do not know there is such a thing as obedience training. They do not know why we prefer sitting to jumping or why it is so important to us that they not move at certain times (stay).

Anyone who lives with a dog should realize that dogs experience the world differently than we do. They focus on information they get through their sense of smell and they communicate with body language. We focus on information we take in through our ears, and we communicate verbally. This difference in perception makes it difficult for us to teach dogs what we want them to learn. We sometimes inadvertently teach our dogs things we didn't want them to learn.

For example, how many people unknowingly teach their dogs to engage in some unwanted behavior, such as jumping, barking, nudging or nipping, by giving the dog attention at the very moment she engages in that behavior? Even if we say, "No, no, bad dog don't do that!" this is rarely sufficient to extinguish the behavior. And in comparison to being bored and ignored, "No, no bad dog!" sounds pretty good.

By developing a clear system of communication with the dog to point out to her the exact behavior we like, we clarify, simplify and speed up the learning process. In addition we reduce the frustration of cross-species communication.

That is why we must clearly and precisely communicate to the dog exactly what she is doing correctly. We must never assume she *knows* what we want or what is good behavior or bad behavior. Dogs do not have the burden of a conscience.

Importance of a Conditioned Reinforcer

A conditioned reinforcer is a very important tool for dog training. It enables you to form a verbal bridge between the correct behavior you are teaching and your unconditioned reinforcer. When you teach your dog to understand a conditioned reinforcer, you will be able to communicate with your dog much more clearly. This will increase the effectiveness of your training.

Remember, whether you are using food, a toy, a walk, petting or anything else, the unconditioned reinforcer *must* be something the *dog* considers rewarding. You can't use a tennis ball if the dog isn't crazy for tennis balls, and you can't use freeze-dried liver if the dog likes cheese better.

How to Train a Conditioned Reinforcer

First you must decide what your conditioned reinforcer signal will be. Some suggestions include:

◆ "Good"

◆ "Yes"

◆ "Excellent"

◆ A whistle

◆ A clicker

Then, you must teach the dog what your selected conditioned reinforcer is. Following are a couple of ways you can do this.

Establish a Conditioned Reinforcer Using a Random Schedule of Reinforcement

This exercise is a very simple one that will enable you to teach your dog a selected conditioned reinforcer. The idea behind this method is to give the dog your conditioned reinforcer ("good") right before you give the dog her unconditioned reinforcer (food). When you do this, the dog will understand the value of the word "good" (the conditioned reinforcer). This understanding will be an invaluable tool for future training.

Step 1: Get 150 to 200 of the very soft and small food treats your dog likes.

Step 2: Begin this exercise only when your dog is hungry.

Step 3: Sit down on the sofa in the living room. Make sure there are no distractions for the dog. Put some treats where you can reach them but the dog cannot (maybe up on the back of the sofa behind you).

Step 4: At random times, say the conditioned reinforcer "good" and toss a treat to the dog. It doesn't matter what the dog is doing when you toss the treat. Watch TV or read a book, so you can ignore the dog long enough between treats so that she leaves you alone and starts to do something else. She may look out the window, sniff around, scratch or sleep. It doesn't matter.

Step 5: After 150 to 200 trials (a trial is one training experience— in this case, saying "good" and tossing a treat), your dog should perk up every time she hears your conditioned reinforcer "good," in antici- pation of the unconditioned reinforcer (food). The word "good" now has a specific meaning to the dog. It means, "I am about to get a treat!"

Step 6: The word "good" can now be maintained as a valuable training tool to communicate to your dog when she did the right thing and exactly how well she did.

Step 7: When you're teaching the dog a command, each correct response should be followed by the word "good," and the best responses should be followed with the dog's unconditioned reinforcer (food).

Vary Your Reinforcement

You should start to vary your reinforcement only after your condi- tioned reinforcer has been properly trained. This will increase your communication with the dog.

For example, if your dog performs a "sit" when she is given the "sit" command, but sits slowly, you may signal your dog that she per- formed the correct behavior by saying "good," but not follow it with any unconditioned reinforcer (in other words, no food). However, if you give your dog a "sit" command and she sits faster that usual, you'd give your conditioned reinforcer "good" at the moment her bottom touches the ground (to mark the aspect of the behavior you liked) and follow it with your unconditioned reinforcer (food).

This will teach her that the faster "sit" was more valuable to you. Over time the dog will do more of the faster sits, since they are the ones that get her the food treat. Slow sits, while a correct response to the "sit" command, have less value to your dog, because "good" is not followed by a food treat.

In fact, you can further hone your communication with the dog by being aware of which unconditioned reinforcers your dog likes better, and only giving those for the most excellent behaviors. For example, the fastest sit gets a piece of steak after "good," while a fast sit gets a piece of cheese after "good." A medium sit gets a cracker after "good" and a slow sit gets nothing after the conditioned reinforcer "good."

You can also make some rewards more valuable by increasing the amount of the reward. A piece of steak is better than a cracker, and three pieces of steak are better than one piece of steak!

My Golden Rule

A dog must only receive the things she likes if she is obedient. This is the No Free Lunch policy.

The best way to train is to teach the dog to work *for* the things she likes, through obedience. If the owner *gives* the dog things she likes *for free,* what is the dog's motivation to be obedient?

Here are some important steps to increase the value of obedience:

Step 1: Follow the No Free Lunch policy.

To do this, you must become aware of all the things your dog likes. These things are the dog's unconditioned reinforcers, and even some self-taught conditioned reinforcers. The family should sit down and make a list. The dog should be required to do at least a simple "sit" before gaining access to *anything* she likes. This No Free Lunch policy is one of the most important concepts I will cover in this book.

A sample list of a dog's reinforcers may be:

◆ Food treats

◆ Playing Frisbee

◆ Fetching a tennis ball

◆ Going for a walk

◆ Going for a ride in a car

◆ Having her ears rubbed

◆ Having her chest scratched

◆ Going out to the backyard

◆ Playing with other dogs

Step 2: Teach a verbal conditioned reinforcer.

The reason you teach the dog a verbal conditioned reinforcer, such as "good," is so you can communicate to your dog, "You just did the right thing and will get something you like for doing that."

Remember, using the word "good" as your conditioned reinforcer is different from general praise like, "Oh, what a good boy you are!" This conditioned reinforcer ("good") serves as a bridge to connect the correct behavior and the reinforcement, and is said at the *moment* the dog does the proper behavior. This conditioned reinforcer, or bridge, must be said after each correct response to let the dog know she gave the correct response to your command.

Initially, you will be following each "good" with an unconditioned reinforcer (such as food), until the dog is at least 90 percent correct in her responses to a particular command. By teaching the dog a conditioned reinforcer, the dog will be just as happy when you say the word "good" as she is when given a food treat, because she will anticipate getting a food treat each time she hears "good."

The word "good" alone will eventually get this positive response, even when you have no food treat to give the dog. The power of the word "good" will need to be "recharged" by following it occasionally (about 25 percent of the time) with an unconditioned reinforcer. Preferably, the unconditioned reinforcers will come after the dog's best responses.

Step 3: Hide the rewards.

As soon as you possibly can, you must learn to hide the rewards you intend to give the dog. Hiding food treats and toys around the house that are out of the dog's reach and awareness is a good way to start. This will enable you to surprise the dog with a reward. Give the dog an obedience command that you feel certain she will obey, then surprise the dog with the reward you have hidden.

For example, give the dog the "sit" command very near to where you have a reward hidden. The dog sits and you say "good." You then release the dog with "OK" and reward the dog with one of the following:

◆ Giving the dog a food treat you had hidden in the room

◆ Playing with the dog using a toy you had hidden in the room

◆ Letting the dog go outside

If you only give the dog the things she likes *after* she obeys, she will look forward to obedience because it always comes before the things she likes.

Step 4: Offer food rewards at random times.

When the dog complies 90 percent of the time to a particular obedience command, you need not follow each "good" with an actual food reward. Be aware of your dog's average obedience level, and only follow "good" with a food reward for better-than-average responses.

The dog will soon notice that only her best obedience gets rewarded. Never fall below a 25-percent reward rate (rewarding the top 25 percent of the dog's responses). If you stick to the No Free Lunch policy and always give food rewards at least 25 percent of the time, you will be amazed at how willing your dog is to be obedient.

If you combine this with proper corrections for disobedience and go back a level following any disobedience, you will have a dog who is reliable and happily obedient for the rest of her life.

Remember, these methods and principles take time to understand and to master. Patience, understanding, practice and love will enable everyone to attain the goals you seek with your pets.

Hopefully, you come away after reading this chapter with a clearer understanding of how dogs learn and what many behavioral terms really mean. If so, please go on to Chapter 4.

YOUR DOG AS A FAMILY MEMBER

For roughly 30,000 years, human beings and dogs have had a fascinating and rewarding relationship. At the core of human-dog interaction are some very interesting similarities. Humans and dogs are both highly social beings with numerous sophisticated communication skills. Both species are group or pack oriented and territorial. Although we were once competitors for food, the relationship between humans and dogs has evolved into a symbiotic one.

A MEMBER OF THE FAMILY

Everyone comes from some kind of family and every family has a structure, with different members having different responsibilities to that group. For thousands of years the roles family members were expected to perform remained fairly consistent. Although family roles today are much less rigid, it's still true that each member has some responsibility to the group. Some members are responsible for financial resources, while others are responsible for taking care of or managing the household. Even small children are responsible for getting an education.

Yet, dogs are kept as pets without any job other than to provide amusement and affection. This is a relatively new development—almost within living memory, common everyday dogs were members of the family with clearly defined roles. They guarded our property, provided personal protection, herded our livestock, rid our households of vermin, helped us hunt, pulled carts and sleds and located lost people.

For the majority of human history, most people had far less disposable income than they do today. There was no dog food industry, and dogs consumed our leftovers. Because houses did not have electronic alarm systems, dogs slept outside to patrol around the house. Because there was no forced or central heating, doors were kept closed as we moved from room to room and only occupied rooms were heated. This meant the dog had to follow us and had no opportunity to move about freely in the house. Because people couldn't afford replacements, household furniture had to last many years, and for this reason dogs were not allowed on the furniture. Because people expected their dogs to work at one of the jobs listed earlier, they were respected members of the family with clearly defined responsibilities, not surrogate children.

Fifty to 75 years ago, some behavior problems commonly seen today in dogs were rarely seen at all. These include nervous disorders, idiopathic aggression, lack of desire to fetch or learn obedience, separation anxiety, incessant and useless barking and severe phobias. One of the biggest reasons we see so many more of these behaviors is that today, most dogs no longer have clearly defined jobs within their family pack.

Unfortunately, and what many dog owners don't realize, is that by failing to give a dog a clearly defined role, you are communicating a lack of leadership and social cohesiveness to the dog. This creates anxiety, which often causes behavior problems.

Today, dogs are frequently treated like the leader of the pack by being allowed to get up on beds and furniture, eating out of an overflowing food bowl whenever they like, coming and going as they please, having lots of unearned possessions to guard, having subordinates fawn over them with constant free petting and being able to demand to be played with, petted, taken out or left alone. This is not how dogs exist in their own packs, and it is bound to cause miscommunication and confusion when it occurs. The tips and exercises outlined here will help your dog regain his rightful place as a respected, responsible member of the family.

Decades ago, behaviorists observed what most dogs owners have known for centuries: Dogs have a definite social hierarchy. Within the normal dog pack, there is a distinct order in which some members have dominant roles and others subordinate ones. Some of the ways in which individual pack members communicate their position with other pack members seem obvious to human observers. Since the social hierarchy concept is familiar in human group interaction, it was both easy and natural for human beings to create dog training methods based on their observations of dog behavior and their own human instincts.

This is where many familiar confrontational training methods came from. The "alpha roll," in which a human physically forces a dog onto his back, is the result of people observing what appeared to be similar behavior among dogs. The "scruff shake" and direct eye stare were also copies of dog behavior and were thought to be the "natural" way to exert your dominance over your dog.

As our understanding of the subtle complexities of dog behavior and interaction increased, we learned that many of the "natural" training methods I've just described mimicked extremely threatening behaviors that a sane dog pack leader would use only as a last resort and not as a way of "training" or relating to his or her followers. Dogs have a much more complex method of "training" and relating to one another that relies on posturing, social ritual and avoiding confrontation.

This is extremely important for people to understand. In the dog world, avoiding confrontation is very important. Dogs understand that if you are injured in a fight and you cannot hunt, forage, breed and travel to get food—you die. Since effective pack leaders only use threatening behaviors as a last resort, how are humans supposed to act? The answer is, we must appear as strong, dependable, consistent, non-confrontational leaders who know the posturing and social rituals that make sense to our dogs.

In truth, if you want your dog to show stable behavior, you must be this type of leader. Some people are uncomfortable with the entire pack leader concept. In their minds, it's archaic. Why does there have to be a leader? Can't everyone be equal, without some members dominating or leading others? What humans need to grasp is that dogs do not understand the concept of equality. In fact, it is extremely stressful to most dogs to be without a leader. Lack of leadership means no pack cohesion. Without pack cohesion, there is no group hunting, protection of weaker members and other activities that are vital to survival. Dogs did not evolve to survive for any length of time on their own. Their strength is in the structure of the pack. With such instincts, it's easy to understand why if a dog sees no leader, he will become extremely stressed and may even instinctively attempt to fill the leadership position himself—because every pack needs a leader to survive.

In a human family (pack), some dogs, if left to their own devices, will attempt to assert leadership in a canine way. When this happens, humans are faced with a variety of behaviors that they consider unacceptable. These include being pushy or aggressive at the front door, attaining the most central and elevated sleeping area, demanding that they not be disturbed when resting, barking excessively, having first dibs on any food or possessions within reach, having the right to defend any food or possessions they come upon, expecting to not be touched in any way they do not like and being able to demand various forms of attention or behaviors from you, their subordinates.

Other dogs will not attempt to establish leadership, but will be anxious and may engage in a host of anxiety-related behavior, including chewing, digging and barking.

Once dog owners understand these concepts, the question is: How do you show your dog that you are a wise, strong and dependable leader in a way that will enable your dog to remain or become a happy, confident and well-adjusted family member?

Here are some simple guidelines that will allow you to show your dog that his humans are good leaders and that he has a responsibility to the family to serve and follow his leaders. Please note: These methods are completely nonconfrontational.

Feeding

1. The dog should have his meal prepared and then set aside while you eat your meal. He can eat after you've finished.
   In the wild, the leader eats first. This is a very easy way to communicate your leadership role to your dog.

2. The dog should wait for you to set his bowl down and give him permission to eat (release with "OK!") before he advances toward his bowl to eat. If you have not attained this level of control through obedience, make sure he is leashed and prevented from advancing toward the bowl until he is released.
   Although there are no leashes in the wild, dogs will understand that this is leadership behavior.

3. The dog must finish his entire meal in one sitting. If he leaves food in his bowl, the food is taken up until the next scheduled meal.
   This prevents the dog from having unlimited access to food, which he would never have in a regular dog pack.

Sleeping

1. The dog should not be allowed to sleep on human beds or human furniture.

2. The dog should sleep outside the bedrooms.
   Another easy way to assert your leadership.

3. The dog should accept being gently moved from any sleeping or resting place.

Access to and Movement Throughout the House

1. Night: Untrained dogs should sleep in a crate. If you want the dog to have free access to the inside of the house at night, that can only be allowed after the dog has house manners (is quiet, calm, obedient, stays off furniture, is housebroken, doesn't touch forbidden objects like shoes or TV remote controls, stays out of forbidden areas of the house and so on). Additionally, you must have

all dog behavior problems (such as aggression or separation anxiety) solved before granting the dog free access at night.

2. Day: Until the puppy or dog has house manners, he should not be allowed loose in the house. The key word here is *loose*. This does not mean owners can't have their puppy in the house. It does mean until he is trained, your dog must be crated or kept on a leash by you. Leaving an untrained dog to run free or unsupervised in your house will likely create numerous problems. For some owners, keeping their dog crated sounds cruel and restrictive. It is not, and while I sympathize, it is important to understand that you won't have to do this forever. Four to six months of crating and consistent training will probably result in a dog who learns to be calm and well behaved in your house. Is it worth half a year to have 15 years (God willing) of calm house behavior? I think so, and I hope you'll agree.

The crate can be a very useful tool in controlling your dog's freedom in the house. If you make the crate a safe haven for your dog by putting toys and occasional treats in it, your dog will likely get used to it and even enjoy being there. However, I think it's important for everyone to understand time frames with regard to crating. That is, how long can you realistically put your dog in a crate? I am not suggesting that owners leave their dogs crated all day long. Quite simply, most dogs will find that intolerable—and who wouldn't?!

This does raise some challenges for owners who don't have anywhere to put their dog during an average workday, when they're gone for six to 10 hours. Believe it or not, I have spoken to numerous trainers about this dilemma and many of them flat out say if you live in an environment with no yard and nowhere to put the dog during the day, and you're working, you shouldn't own a dog. I disagree. In my mind, while this situation is not ideal, it's the reality many people live with. So what can you do? There are several options.

If you are gone all day, you may consider a house sitter, or at the very least a dog walking service. I've worked with people who crated their dogs for a number of months until they were trained.

The dog was crated when they left first thing in the morning. However, they had a dog walker take the dog out two or three times a day while they were gone. This meant the dog was not crated for longer than three or four hours at a time. Some people have used pet sitters, although the cost of having someone there from nine to five, Monday through Friday, for many months makes this option too expensive for most people. Additionally, if you're going this route, the pet sitter needs to follow the same training regimen you do, or you'll never get anywhere with your training.

Many owners overcome the crating challenge by getting home for lunch. If you have kids who are old enough to be trusted with the responsibility, the children can exercise the dog and handle portions of the training when they get home from school. Many owners make this a cooperative family effort. Some enlist the help of trusted neighbors or relatives living nearby. In my experience, if an owner genuinely wants to get someone to take their dog out a couple of times a day when they're gone, it usually happens.

If you absolutely can't get this covered, please consider the crating instructions found in Chapter 6 for housebreaking and paper training. Basically, instead of a crate, you'll need an exercise pen, because the pen can be made larger and less confining than a crate. If you're housebreaking at the same time you're addressing unruly behavior, there are other tools you'll need that are covered in that portion of this book.

Please note that young puppies may find it very difficult to avoid eliminating for longer than three to six hours. A good guide is to expect an hour of control for every month of a puppy's life. That is, a three-month-old puppy can hold it for three hours, a four-month-old for four hours, etc. If your dog eliminates in the crate, you may have confined him too long. Remember, the crate should be large enough for your dog to comfortably lie in, but not so huge that he can walk all the way to the other side and be well out of the way of any mess he may have made in the crate. If you are unsure, contact a local professional trainer.

3. Before the puppy or dog learns house manners, he should be given an on-leash "tour" each time he enters or is allowed to walk

through the house. Calmly walk the puppy through the house on a leash and head collar, allowing him to sniff. Praise and reward him with food treats for being calm. If he tries to drag you through the house, simply stop and wait for him to focus back on you. If he sticks his nose somewhere it shouldn't be (for example, in a potted plant, shoes, children's toys), gently pull the dog away from it and continue with your tour. Don't use your voice to interrupt him. You don't want him to think he should only leave those things alone around you! Remember to reward calm behavior. Please don't attempt to bring your puppy in the house if you are not sure when he last relieved himself or if he hasn't had sufficient exercise to be able to be calm in the house.

Many of you are familiar with the "puppy crazies" that afflict most puppies several times each day. This is when your dog starts running around grabbing things and generally acting wild and rambunctious. There is nothing wrong or unusual about this behavior. However, it is generally not something you should encourage or reward in the house. If the "puppy crazies" strike while he's in the house, it is definitely time to take him outside for exercise. If your puppy already has a habit of being rambunctious and playing in the house, it will take longer for him to learn the new rules of being calm in the house.

Be patient and consistent when teaching your dog house manners and he'll catch on. Remember, consistency is critical in training. This means avoid playing rambunctious, high-energy games with your dog in the house. These include fetch and chase games.

4. After your tour of the house has concluded, you can recrate the puppy or teach him to go to a safe spot. To do this, take the puppy to a well-trafficked area of the house and work on teaching him a safe spot exercise.

   Safe spot exercise: Attach the leash to a secure object, thus preventing the puppy from being able to wander around the house. The puppy should be wearing a buckle-type collar when he's secured, not a choke chain or head collar. Additionally, NEVER attach the leash to an object or near an object that the puppy can jump over. Dogs have been known to hang themselves over the backs of chairs, couches and fences. Be careful! Never leave your dog on a leash unattended. Finally, if your puppy chews on the leash, treat it with chew repellent or use a chain leash. If you have a mat for him to lie on, place it where you want him to lie down. Give the puppy an appropriate chew toy he enjoys and invite him to lie down and relax in that area on his mat. Again, reward calm behavior. (Incidentally, you can start telling him "go to your place" as you are taking him to his mat, so eventually, you can tell him from anywhere in the house to "go to your place" and he'll go there by himself.)

In the beginning, be careful not to work on this safe spot exercise for more than five to 30 minutes at a time. When he knows some simple commands, if he starts to get fussy you can, in an unemotional and calm way, tell him "no" and give him the "down" command. If this doesn't settle him, ask yourself if the puppy was properly prepared to be in the house. Does he need to relieve himself? Has he had sufficient exercise? Don't get into an argument or start struggling with him. If he doesn't calm down after you've given the "down" command, it might be best to take him outside and try the safe spot exercise again later. But before you try again later, you will likely need to recrate him or put him outside. This is not punishment. He will soon learn, if you are consistent, that being rambunctious gets him put outside or crated and being calm allows him to stay in the house in a comfortable spot, surrounded by toys.

5. After your puppy understands the routine of the calm tour, followed by going to his safe spot to lie down, you can start training him to have small amounts of freedom in the house.

6. Begin teaching the puppy boundary training techniques. The idea is for the dog to learn there are a few areas of the house that are off-limits. The bedrooms, or at least the master bedroom, are excellent off-limits areas. As you take him on his tour, show him that doors to these areas will always close if he starts to enter those rooms uninvited. Be careful not to close any of the doors on

your dog because that could hurt him. Simply make sure that if the dog starts to enter an off-limits area, you pull the dog back and close the door or have someone on the other side of the door close it while you pull your dog back. If this is done consistently, your dog will get the message in a couple of weeks. This can be further reinforced when he has learned enough obedience, because you can then practice sit-stays and down-stays on the correct side of those doorways.

7. Eventually, allow your puppy to be somewhat off-leash in the same room with you. Start by leaving the leash on and allowing him to drag it around. Only do this when your full attention is on him, so you can catch the puppy the instant he starts to act inap-propriately (for example, putting paws on furniture, chewing plants, shoes or toys). If the dog does act inappropriately, inter-rupt the behavior with a gentle pull of the leash and then redirect his attention to one of his toys if he was chewing inappropriately or put him back in his spot if he was jumping on the furniture. If he needs to relieve himself, take him outside to eliminate. It's important to make sure your puppy is always wearing his leash in the house until several weeks have passed in which you have not had to correct any inappropriate behavior. Until that time, the leash should always be worn because it gives you the opportunity to address numerous unacceptable behaviors. For example, if he suddenly leaps up on the sofa, you can calmly walk over, grab the leash and whisk him off the sofa. Lead him away from the sofa and after three to five seconds, praise him for being on the floor.

8. Gradually increase his freedom as he earns it. One mistake and you should take a step backward—go back to freedom in just one room, such as the kitchen, for shorter periods of time with the leash dragging. Most dog owners go too fast in giving their puppy freedom. Remember, you wouldn't allow a two-year-old child to run around unsupervised. Most dogs can't handle being loose in the house for even an hour until they are eight to 10 months old.

Remember, never leave your dog on a leash unattended.

Playing

1. First, select appropriate play and chew toys for your dog. I am grouping play and chew toys together because you should play with your dog with his chew toys, especially in the beginning.

◆ Acceptable Chew or Play Toys

◇ Kong or Rhino toys

◇ Nylabones

◇ Hard rubber balls like Boomer Balls that are large enough that they won't get stuck in your dog's throat; better too large than too small

◇ Soft flying disks (think fabric Frisbee-type disks)

◇ Interactive play toys like the Buster Cube, a square box you can put little food treats in; by moving it around, your dog can get some of the treats. Many dogs spend hours playing with this toy.

Nylabone makes excellent chew bones
in many shapes, sizes and flavors.

COURTESY KONG

The Kong is a great play toy and is very helpful in addressing many dog problems.

No dog should have free access to a play toy. Free access to possessions tells a dog that he is the leader. Also, it gives the dog an opportunity to destroy and ingest these toys, which can be dangerous.

◆ Unacceptable Play Toys

◇ Don't use tennis balls and stuffed fuzzy toys. These are too similar to unacceptable items, like your carpeting and clothing.

◇ Ropes or other toys for tug-of-war can stimulate some dogs to be aggressive. They're an absolute no-no for households with children.

◇ Most squeaky rubber toys can be chewed into little pieces, which presents a health risk for the dog.

2. Get your dog focused on the appropriate play and chew toys. This is done by making the toys a major source of interaction between you and the dog. Play with the dog and his toys. Greet him with his toys. Act coy with his toys. Constantly focusing him on his

COURTESY KONG

Dogs love Kongs.

toys and praising him when he plays with them will soon result in your dog seeking the toys out on his own. When he seeks them out, praise this behavior. Some owners dismiss certain toys, like Kongs or Nylabones, saying, "My dog doesn't like that toy." This is because the dog has not been properly focused on them. Try soaking the Nylabone in beef or chicken broth and filling the Kong with cheese or peanut butter. You could get your dog to love to play with a cast iron skillet if you came home from work each day, grabbed the skillet, ran around with it, buried it, smeared it with liver or peanut butter and basically made it the center of all your positive interactions with the dog. In other words, focusing your dog on the correct toys makes them the signal for tasty treats, interaction and fun with you! (By the way, please don't try this with a skillet. It will save your dog's teeth and keep my hate mail to a minimum.)

3. One of the best games for you to play with your dog is fetch. The right way to play fetch with your dog is for you to decide to start

the game with a toy that is in your possession. You toss the toy and give the "fetch" command. The dog brings the toy back to you and drops it at your feet or in your hand, either automatically or on command. If your dog has little or no desire to fetch, runs off with the toy, tries to get you to chase him, refuses to give it back or decides he suddenly doesn't want to play anymore, simply stop playing the game for 10 to 15 minutes. You can also try a variation of this called the two-toy game, which is found in Chapter 5.

4. Other acceptable ways to play with your dog involve teaching obedience and tricks. Think about this for a second: Why should your dog associate obedience with work? What if your dog considered it play? Perhaps your dog would be far more inclined to listen. A simple obedience exercise that many dogs find fun is hiking with your dog in a safe open area. Many dogs will start by following or walking with you, but quickly get distracted and move off on their own. When your dog does, don't say a word. Instead, simply walk in the opposite direction until your dog, looking up from whatever he was doing, runs to follow you. As soon as he reaches you, praise him and continue to walk. This exercise is a great way to encourage your dog to follow you outside without a leash. This also teaches your dog in a very non-confrontational way that you are the leader, because every time your dog follows you, the message of your leadership is communicated in a very positive way. Remember, you need a safe, enclosed area at least half the size of a football field to do this exercise effectively. This is much different than walking down a sidewalk, where most people end up following their dog. Another option is hide-and-seek, where your dog must find you, another member of your family, or a toy you have hidden from him.

5. Unacceptable ways of playing with your dog include teasing, slapping, wrestling, chasing, allowing him to bark at you to demand that you play with him, using your hands as a toy, allowing him to nip, and tug-of-war.

Positive Obedience

Positive obedience should be incorporated into your daily activities. Positive obedience is obedience the dog does to get something (such as petting, a car ride, a treat, a walk, play with a toy). Most people give their dog all those things for free and then only use obedience as a way to control their dog when he is either about to do something wrong or already has. Then they punish him if he doesn't obey. The dog soon figures out that if he can just avoid the punishing consequences of misbehaving by moving fast or adopting a pathetic look, he has it made. This is why making obedience fun is a much better way to train. It's also a great deal more rewarding for you, since almost no one likes harsh, repetitive obedience that's as much work for the trainer as it is for the dog.

An Important Professional Tip

Most owners ignore their dogs when they are being good. This is understandable, because it is much easier to ignore a dog who is sitting quietly by your side or a dog lying on his mat in the safe spot than a dog who is jumping on you or running madly through the house with a dish towel in his mouth. Because of this, most dogs quickly figure out that doing something bad is what gets them attention. For a social animal like a dog, negative attention is better than no attention at all.

A good example of this is when dogs jump up on people. When observing a jumping dog, dog trainers typically see an active, intelligent dog who is jumping up as a greeting gesture. The dog has learned that standing or sitting quietly will not get him the attention he is seeking, so the dog tries the next thing that comes to his mind to get attention—jumping. This works every time! The owners turn to look at him, talk to him ("No, no don't do that!") and touch him (by trying to push him away). Looking at, talking to and touching are what trainers call *reinforcing*; in other words, those actions will tend to reward the dog and increase the likelihood the dog will do them again. The dog ends up thinking jumping is a game and the owners get frustrated. Even if the owner is able to administer a strong enough correction to deter the jumping, the dog will still try to get attention, and some dogs will then resort to looking for "safe" times to jump, such as jumping straight up instead of on you or jumping on your back. Other dogs may engage in what is sometimes called *symptom substitution*, which is a fancy way of saying they'll engage in a different unacceptable behavior to get your attention. Some of these include barking at you, whining, grabbing their leash or stealing whatever object they can find that will get your attention (a shoe, the TV remote control, a child's toy or a dish towel).

To effectively teach your dog to be good by rewarding good behavior, you must also train yourself to be on the lookout for your dog's good behavior. Remind yourself and your family members to give the dog praise, attention and treats when he's being good. Do this consistently and your dog will be far less motivated to engage in bad behaviors to get attention.

Continuing to use jumping as an example, the next step in learning how to train your dog to get attention by being good is to prove to him that every time he approaches any person and sits, he will get attention and a reward. If he suddenly stands up or jumps, simply turn away until he sits down again.

After the dog has had several weeks of consistently being rewarded for sitting any time he is near a person, he will learn that the appropriate way to greet people is to sit, as opposed to jump. The final step is to teach your dog that no matter what a person does, the dog should sit when he's near them. Set up situations where people come and tap their chest and invite him to jump. They can also throw their hands up and speak excitedly to him. The instant the dog jumps, the attention stops and the person turns away. After 20 or 30 seconds, most dogs will sit, especially if the sit behavior has been consistently reinforced over several weeks in numerous situations. The instant the dog sits, praise this appropriate behavior. Following these directions consistently will teach your dog that jumping is not rewarding and sitting is the appropriate way to greet people.

Jumping is used as the example here for discussing attention, but it is easy to use these techniques to eliminate any other undesirable behavior your dog engages in to get attention.

FINAL THOUGHTS

If you read this chapter and come away with a better understanding of what your role in your dog's world needs to be, you are on your way to a better relationship with your pet. If you come away also understanding some specific ways to communicate your role in a nonphysical, nonaggressive way, you are ready to move to the next level. Please read the Practical Training Rules that follow before moving on. And if you are unclear about anything in this chapter, please read it again.

PRACTICAL TRAINING RULES

1. If a training method is ineffective, it doesn't matter how good it sounds.

2. Communication is critical, as is understanding.

3. Reward exists in nature; so does punishment.

4. Reward is more effective in teaching desired behavior than punishment.

5. It's much better to teach your dog what you want him to do than to focus on what you don't want him to do.

6. To address a behavior problem effectively, you must understand its cause.

7. Never correct in anger.

8. Do nothing to physically harm your dog.

9. *No training method works for every dog.*

CHAPTER 5

SIMPLE, EFFECTIVE WAYS TO ADDRESS BASIC PROBLEMS, PART 1

Whenever I teach class, I start off with a review of the commands we are going to cover in the program. I then discuss what equipment each student will need to successfully train their dog. I also make it a point to ask each owner what breed or type of dog they will be bringing (my first group lessons are typically without the dogs). After sharing a little breed knowledge with the rest of the class, I then open up the floor for any questions the students may have. Without fail, almost all the questions I am asked concern problem behaviors. These include: How do I stop my dog from jumping up on people? My dog nips and mouths on my hands and feet. My dog is a maniac when she comes in the house, barks excessively, steals food off counters, eats my furniture, is tearing up my yard, etc.

The truth is, far more people enroll in training classes to address behavior problems than they do to teach their dogs basic commands. For this reason, chapters 5 and 6 of this book are devoted to helping you solve or curtail many of the common behaviors that dog owners find challenging.

These methods have worked with millions of people and are tried and tested. Remember, no method works for every dog. In addition, for training to be effective, it must be done consistently.

GOALS

These are the goals for this chapter:

1. Identify the problem you wish to address.
2. Learn the solutions to the behavior problem you wish to solve.
3. Apply the solution with patience, consistency, understanding and love.

Here are the problems I'll cover in this chapter:

- Jumping
- Puppy nipping and mouthing
- Unruly behavior in the house
- Begging food from the table
- Stealing food from counters
- Jumping on furniture
- Excessive barking

JUMPING

When addressing a jumping problem, it is important not to do anything that may make it worse or create other problems. As with all training, you need to give your dog a consistent message about jumping: specifically that jumping is not a desired behavior. Many owners don't realize that they give their dogs mixed messages. For example, do you play in a rough, excited way with your dog, accepting the inevitable jumping that comes with this kind of play, but when you're dressed for work, discourage the exact same jumping behavior? If your answer is yes, this causes confusion and even anxiety in your pet.

This is why it's important to avoid rough games and excitable greetings, because these types of interactions encourage jumping. Owners who teach their dogs that jumping is acceptable some times but not other times will almost always have difficulty eliminating the problem. When you're interacting with a dog who tends to jump, greet and interact with her in a calm and gentle fashion. Most important, teach the dog alternative, acceptable ways to greet you. This cannot be overstated. Earlier, I mentioned that punishment or correction has a place in training. Now I'm going to share something even more important.

It is far more effective to praise and reward proper behavior than it is to correct improper behavior.

Remember the old saying, "You attract more bees with honey." This is relevant in dealing with jumping! You need to teach, praise and reward your dog for greeting you the right way.

Consider teaching your dog to sit as a form of greeting and to play fetch instead of leaping all over you. Remember, jumping is primarily a play and greeting behavior. Also remember that although jumping is unacceptable in dog-human interactions, it is normal and acceptable behavior between dogs. This is another reason why it is so important to avoid encouraging it at any time.

Be prepared before you play with your puppy. Always have several toys and treats on hand. Instead of playing roughly, which includes wrestling and vigorous petting, direct the dog's attention to her proper toys.

A good way to get your dog to focus on proper toys is to teach her to play fetch. This can be accomplished with what I call the two-toy game. It involves taking two toys at a time and teaching the dog to fetch them. Get the dog to focus on one of the toys and then toss that toy across the room. When the dog runs over and grabs it, pull out the other one and focus the dog's attention on that toy. Encourage her to come toward you by coaxing her with the second toy. When she runs over to you, take the first toy from her and then toss the second toy. If the dog is reluctant to give up the first toy, trade her for a food treat. Use the food treats consistently until the dog understands that the faster she drops the first toy, the quicker she gets a treat and you throw the second toy for her. When she willingly and consistently gives up the first toy, you may start to slowly eliminate the food treats. Remember, if the puppy gets too wound up and starts to jump, tone the game down or stop playing.

If this game is played while the puppy is wearing a leash and head collar, you can easily stop the jumping with a gentle tug of the leash the moment she jumps. Please note, I said "gentle tug." Then wait until the puppy has been calm for two long seconds before resuming the game. Also remember, *never* let your dog wear a leash or head collar unattended.

A word about head collars: This is one of the things that has changed in the last few decades and, in my opinion, changed for the better. In most cases head collars are far more effective for controlling behaviors like jumping than collars worn around the dog's neck. The reason is that you can control the dog's head and body more effectively and with less force using a head collar.

When she jumps, simply say "no" and gently tug the leash. The head collar makes this correction easy to administer. Hold the dog's head and body away from you until the dog is visibly calmer and not jumping. Then allow her to greet you again. If she reapproaches you without jumping, praise her. This technique can be extremely effective with most dogs, provided you are consistent and the dog wears the leash and head collar whenever you interact with her. However, if she only wears it half the time, you will likely wind up with a dog who only behaves when she's on a leash.

Teach other people interacting with your puppy how to greet her properly, so they do not inadvertently encourage jumping behavior. Make sure the dog's primary handlers greet her properly with hands kept slow and low and excitable greetings avoided.

Once you've addressed the issue of not encouraging jumping behavior with your greetings and play, the next step in eliminating the jumping problem is to focus on praising appropriate greeting behaviors. This is accomplished by encouraging and rewarding proper behaviors whenever you can. Coax your dog to you and reward her for sitting when she gets there. This should be done every time you greet your dog. If it is, most dogs will learn to greet you by sitting in two to four weeks.

A question I often hear is: How do I teach my dog to sit?

There are several ways to get the dog into a sitting position, including holding a piece of food two to four inches over the top of the dog's head and slowly bringing it back toward her rear. This will encourage most dogs to sit. The food treat can be given after the dog has been in the sit position for two seconds.

Another method involves gently placing the dog into the sit position by holding the collar with one hand and gently pushing the dog's rump down with the other hand, as you pull up slightly with the hand holding the collar. Praise the dog after she has been sitting for two seconds. The key here is to encourage and reward the sit response whenever possible. The stronger the sit behavior is, the more likely the dog will sit when greeting owner, family and friends.

Consistently give the dog an appropriate negative consequence for jumping. One negative consequence is for the dog to lose her playmate. When the dog jumps, turn away and instantly stop all interaction with her. Most dogs will continue to jump for 15 or 20 seconds before trying something else. Usually they will come around to face you and then jump again. If this happens, turn the other way and continue to ignore the behavior. Make sure you do not touch the dog with your hands or look down at the dog at this time, as the dog may interpret those behaviors as rewarding.

You may need to ignore the dog like this for up to two or three minutes before the dog stops jumping and tries another approach. Other approaches may be to bring a toy or to sit. If your dog tries any of these approaches, instantly praise her. Be careful to avoid praising the dog too excitedly, as that may stimulate more jumping. If, after two or three minutes, the jumping has not stopped, you may need to walk away from the dog. This means literally walking out of the room and not allowing the dog to follow you. After two or three minutes you can return, and may be surprised to find that your dog greets you in a far more subdued fashion.

The method I've just described takes a nonphysical approach to eliminating jumping. The primary focus is praising the dog for engaging in appropriate behavior. This can be highly effective. However, it is not always effective and is not for everyone. For owners training large dogs with long nails, owners with small children or elderly people who may be unsteady on their feet, this may not be the best method.

Other techniques involve saying "no" the instant the dog jumps. This "no" command is followed by a physical correction that is sufficient to stop the jumping behavior. The type of correction needed may be different for every dog. A leash correction is a gentle tug on the leash in a downward motion. Remember, the head collar greatly increases the effectiveness of leash corrections. You can also gently push the dog away from you. Another correction involves lightly squirting the dog with water. I have found this correction to sometimes work, although I remember a case involving some Labrador Retrievers who were great fans of water and loved being squirted. In fact, they would deliberately jump just to get wet! You may need to try several different corrections to find the one that is most effective for your dog. If a particular correction does not work in a couple of tries, stop using it and try another.

It's very important to remember that after saying "no" and correcting the jumping, the dog must be encouraged to sit and then praised for this appropriate alternative behavior.

Guests present another challenge. Although some guests may be cooperative and patient enough to ignore the dog, most will not be enthusiastic about allowing a dog who isn't theirs to jump all over them for two minutes while they ignore the behavior. A good way to handle guests is to first understand that until the dog learns to properly greet you and immediate family members, it is unlikely she will greet your guests properly. Once she has learned to greet her family properly, the dog should be put on a leash and head collar whenever she greets new people. To accomplish this, hang a spare leash and collar by the front door so that when a guest arrives you can instantly put your dog on the leash. Then invite the guest into your home, encouraging the dog to sit the moment the guest walks in. When the dog sits, the behavior should be praised by both you and your guest. If the dog jumps on the guest, say "no," gently tug the leash to pull the dog off the guest, encourage the dog to sit and then praise her when she does.

If, every time the dog jumps she hears "no" and receives a negative consequence for this behavior, and every time she sits she gets praise, most dogs will learn to sit and not jump. There is nothing cruel about this technique, and it has worked for millions of dog owners.

Basic obedience exercises like sit-stay and down-stay around distractions will teach the dog to focus on you and develop some impulse control. This will teach her that she doesn't have to react to every movement people make, and will be rewarded with treats and praise for not reacting.

It is especially important for the dog to get plenty of practice at the front door. Initially, practice when there are no visitors. Get the dog used to your opening and closing the front door. Then graduate to knocking on the front door and ringing the doorbell many times each day, while the dog is in a sit-stay at the front door. These practice lessons will teach the dog to be calmer when you open the door, making it easier to teach the dog to remain in her sit-stay when guests come through the front door. Practicing this routine at the front door several times each day will not only decrease jumping, it will also lessen the dog's excitement in general, which helps reduce excessive barking at the front door.

Finally, please remember that jumping is a normal behavior and one that will not be eliminated overnight. Some of your dogs may have jumped on you or guests thousands of times, and to expect that any training method will be successful after two or three tries is not realistic. It could take several weeks or as long as a month to curtail a difficult jumping problem. You need to have patience, practice often and be consistent. If you are, you will be able to deal with this and all problems over time.

PUPPY NIPPING AND MOUTHING

When dealing with a nipping or mouthing problem, it is important not to do anything that may make it worse or create other problems. It is critical to give the dog a consistent message that nipping is unacceptable.

To accomplish this, avoid rough games like play-slapping and wrestling with the dog. Also avoid rough or vigorous petting, especially around the face. When interacting with a nippy dog, keep your hands slow and pet the dog in a gentle fashion. Owners of nippy dogs should also avoid tug-of-war games. All these types of interactions encourage nipping. Since nipping is normal behavior among dogs, it is very important to consistently remind your dog that nipping humans is unacceptable. Owners who teach their dogs that nipping is acceptable some times but not others will have a difficult time eliminating the problem.

Whenever possible, make sure nippy, active puppies get *plenty* of exercise. Some puppies nip because they don't have other acceptable ways to burn off energy. This is why proper exercise is a great way to curtail nipping. It is also wise to teach the dog to play fetch games, as this is a great energy burner. Teaching the puppy to fetch will help her learn that it is acceptable and fun to put her mouth on her toys, as opposed to your skin.

Be prepared before you play with your puppy by always having several toys and treats on hand. If you play with your dog with your hands, she will use and view your hands as toys. Direct the dog's attention to proper toys such as hard rubber and vinyl chew toys and interactive toys like Buster Cubes.

As I said in the section on jumping, teach the dog to play fetch. A good fetch game involves encouraging the dog to fetch using two toys at a time. (I have explained how to teach this game on page 75.) Remember, if the puppy gets too wound up and starts to nip, give a leash correction, tone the game down or stop playing altogether.

Another good game to play is hide-and-seek. In this game, you encourage the dog to find you by hiding and calling her name. When she finds you, praise and reward her. This game is even better when a second person is also hiding. As soon as they hear the dog being praised and rewarded for finding you, this person can call and encourage the dog to find them. The game also teaches the dog to associate positive things with coming when called. Here too, avoid getting the dog too excited and stop the game if the dog starts to nip.

Teach people interacting with your puppy to greet her properly so they do not encourage mouthing or nipping. Hands should be kept slow and low. A treat held in one hand can be used to focus the dog's attention while she's petted gently with the other. This will teach the dog to associate positive things with being petted and not nipping. If the dog nips at any time, immediately stop the food reward. You can also have one or two toys on hand to redirect the dog's attention if she becomes overly excited.

The instant the puppy puts her mouth on human skin, the person involved should freeze. This is very important and may take a little practice, since it is a natural reaction to pull away when nipped. Once you freeze, say "off" or "no." While it is not necessary to yell, a sharp tone is acceptable. Most puppies will take their mouths away, look at you and/or back away a bit. After two to three seconds of no nipping, gently and calmly praise the non-nipping response. If the puppy starts to nip again, repeat the process. If, after two or three times, the puppy continues to nip, give the dog a few minutes of time-out by walking away from her.

Although this may seem a passive way to address this problem, it can communicate a powerful message to the dog. That message is, "I will not interact with you when you're too rough." After several minutes you may approach and resume playing with the dog, provided the dog does not start nipping again Do not tolerate or continue to play with a mouthing puppy even if she is tiny and the bites don't hurt.

Some dogs do not respond acceptably or at all when you freeze and say "no" or "off." If this is the case, consider other methods. Try spraying your hands, feet and clothes with an anti-chewing spray. This spray is a bitter-tasting substance that most dogs will not like, and is available in most pet supply stores. Although it sounds mean, I have found the spray is much more effective when sprayed in the dog's mouth the very first time it is used. This means before spraying it on your hands or feet for the *first time*. You will only need to spray it in the dog's mouth once, and it will likely help the dog develop a strong aversion to the taste, making it far more effective when you spray it on your hands and feet.

Bitter Apple and Fooey are two examples
of products that can be used to address
nipping and chewing challenges.

A little planning will go a long way if you're using this method. Most owners have an idea of when their dogs will nip—common times include when you come home after work, when you sit down on the couch to watch TV at night or when you go out in the backyard. If you can identify scenarios in which nipping is likely to occur, you can more easily and consistently spray your hands and feet before the nipping happens. It is also important to keep the spray accessible whenever you are interacting with your dog, so it can be applied quickly, if needed.

Another way to address this problem is to put the dog on a leash and head collar whenever you interact with her. If you're worried about her chewing the leash, use a chain link leash. In most cases, head collars are far more effective than collars worn around the dog's neck for controlling behaviors like nipping. This is because you can control the dog's head (including her teeth) more effectively and with less force using a head collar.

When she nips, say "no" and gently tug the leash. The head harness makes this easy to do. Hold the dog's head away from your body until the dog is visibly calmer. Then put your hands or feet back toward the dog's mouth, avoiding fast movements. If she sniffs or nuzzles, both of which are appropriate greetings, calmly praise her. This technique can be extremely effective with certain puppies, provided you are consistent. If the dog wears the leash whenever you interact with her, you will be fine. However, if she only wears it half the time, you will likely wind up with a dog who only behaves when she's on a leash.

Basic obedience exercises like sit-stay and down-stay around distractions will teach the dog to focus on you and to develop some of the impulse control needed to deter nipping. It is important to practice obedience exercises around the very distractions and activities you know make the puppy want to nip. This type of practice will teach her that she doesn't have to react to every movement people make, and will be rewarded with treats and praise for not reacting.

You may also be able to prevent a lot of nipping by exercising the puppy before any petting or interaction. A tired puppy is much less likely to nip.

Remember that nipping, like jumping, is a normal canine behavior and will not be eliminated overnight. Your dog may have nipped thousands of times, and to expect that any training method will be successful after two or three applications is not realistic. It could take several weeks or as long as a month to curtail a difficult nipping problem. You need to have patience, to practice and to be consistent. If you are, you will be able to deal with this and all problems over time.

UNRULY BEHAVIOR IN THE HOUSE

Consistency is extremely important when you're teaching a dog to have a calm attitude in the house. If you play chase or fetch, or wrestle with the dog in the house and encourage the dog to engage in unruly behavior inside, this is going to make it much more difficult for the dog to learn to be calm in the house. Managing your dog's activities inside by keeping her on a leash will reduce the opportunities she has to misbehave.

As you begin to train your dog to be calm in the house, make sure the dog is getting enough exercise, especially before allowing her to move around freely inside. Otherwise, you are going to find it more difficult to teach calm behavior.

Most people underestimate their dog's exercise requirements. I've seen owners whose dogs live in the backyard most of the time. These owners are often faced with a vicious circle: They would bring their dog in if the dog behaved, but because the dog doesn't, they leave her out. This makes the dog more excited when she's brought in, which causes the owner to leave the dog out. Additionally, they assume that because their dog is fairly energetic, she is going to get all the exercise she needs when she's left alone in the yard. This is usually not true. What's more, as dogs get a little bit older, they often have a very human attitude toward exercise—you know the old joke: Whenever I feel like exercising, I lie down until the feeling passes. Often the only thing that causes dogs to become active is a new situation that excites them, such as coming into the house. The bottom line here is, take the dog for long walks, give the dog some exercise, play with your dog in the yard, and you will find it easier to deal with this problem.

To begin teaching your dog to come in calmly, you will need to put your dog on a leash and head collar every single time you let your dog inside. I stress, *every single time.* That means when you bring the dog in, if 10 minutes later you need to take the dog out to go to the bathroom, when you bring the dog back inside again, even if it is only five minutes after that, the dog goes back on the leash. You must be consistent with this.

When you bring her in, slowly walk the dog through the house. Have some food treats available to reward the dog when she is being calm, especially if she walks calmly by something that ordinarily excites her. If, for example, you bring her in and she sees the cat—which would normally stimulate her to go crashing through the house—as long as she is not trying to drag you, definitely reward and praise her. After the initial tour, take the dog to a well-trafficked area and safely tie her to a suitable object. Use a chain link leash to prevent her from chewing through the leash. Give the dog a comfortable pad to lie on and a nice chew toy. Give her food rewards, petting and praise, when she is quiet.

Never leave the dog unattended on a leash or a head collar. Also, make sure when you tie the dog to something in the house that you do not tie her in such a way that she could jump up or over it and hang herself. Be very careful about tying the dog, and never leave the dog unattended when she is tied to something.

Give extra rewards when the dog remains calm even though something exciting is happening around her. For example, she is lying calmly, chewing her toy, when suddenly the kids come running into the room; if she still remains reasonably calm, praise and reward her. What do I mean by "reasonably calm"? She may look up from chewing her toy. She may even stand up. But, as long as she does not start barking, jumping three feet in the air or generally going crazy (remember, she is tied to something), praise and reward her. Remember not to praise her in a way that makes her wild.

Trainers know that *positive reinforcement of a desired behavior will strengthen that behavior.* Actually, positive reinforcement of any behavior will strengthen that behavior. One of the things you want to remember is not to inadvertently reward inappropriate behaviors. That is one of the reasons you should bring the dog inside on a leash. Look at what typically happens when you bring your dog inside unleashed. The dog crashes through the house like a maniac, and what is your response? Often it is to chase after the dog, which then encourages the dog to run and the whole thing becomes a big game. Even though you are not deliberately reinforcing this wild behavior, the dog is thinking, "Wow, they let me in the house and then they chased me all over the place. This is fun!"

If the dog cannot be calm in the house, or gets excited after a calm period and you cannot calm her back down, simply take her outside or put her in her crate.

As soon as possible, teach the dog some simple obedience commands and add these commands to the tour you give the dog whenever she enters the house. Obedience is very important and can be useful when dealing with this behavior problem. In fact, over time, using the "stay" and "down" commands, you will be able to teach your dog to go to a specific spot in a room and lie down. This can really come in handy if you want your dog to be well mannered in the house.

As soon as the dog knows some obedience commands, you can use these commands when your dog becomes disruptive. Calmly tell the dog "no" and give the dog a series of obedience commands to get her back under control. Make sure you give the dog plenty of praise for responding correctly to any obedience command. Simply put, getting better control of the dog, giving the dog exercise and teaching the dog to come in calmly by walking the dog through the house on a leash and head collar will enable you to address unruly house behavior.

Unruliness at home is a relatively simple problem, but if untreated, owners often experience a snowball effect. Here is a story I have heard more than once: "I have a dog I would love to bring into the house, but I don't because the dog misbehaves. So I leave the dog out in the back-yard, and when I go out to greet the dog she jumps all over me because she doesn't see me all that often. This makes me not want to spend as much time with the dog, which makes the dog crazier."

The problem here is that after six months of this, the dog is spending 23½ out of 24 hours each day out in the backyard. Dogs are social animals, just like people. This means that when left to their own devices, dogs will instinctively look for others of their own kind and establish some sort of a social bond. Dogs are not comfortable being outcasts and being by themselves all the time. This means your dog needs companionship in order to remain emotionally stable. Yet, because the dog misbehaves and her owners lack the knowledge to modify the unwanted behavior, the dog doesn't get the social contact she needs for proper development. Some dogs, in circumstances like this, jump fences. Other dogs bark excessively. Still other dogs dig, chew or engage in separation anxiety behavior. This is why many dogs end up homeless and in shelters.

Now, I am not saying that you have to teach the dog to come in calmly or you are going to have a separation anxiety problem. Just understand the correlation here and make sure you teach your dog proper behavior so that she can get the social contact she needs to remain happy and emotionally stable.

BEGGING FOOD FROM THE TABLE

To solve this problem, you need to show the dog what you would like her to do during your meals. The simplest way to do that is to establish a spot near the dining area that your dog learns to like going to. Since the spot will not be at the table, it will not be possible for your dog to beg and be in her spot at the same time.

The key is for your dog to learn to love being in this spot. This will take a little time but is well worth the effort. To accomplish this, make it a point to take your dog to this spot five or six times a day. Once there, safely leash the dog and give her a special toy to play with. Praise her when she chews it and remains calm in the spot. For the first week don't have the dog in the spot during meals, leave her in the backyard. During the second week, sit at the table along with the rest of the family while she is in her spot so that she gets used to this, but still avoid having her there during meals. If you do this correctly and consistently, by the third week, your dog will be comfortable lying quietly in her spot while the family sits at the table. At this point, you can start to have her in her spot during meals. Remember to keep the whole experience positive.

Even after several weeks, some dogs will whine or bark when leashed during meals. To eliminate this, start off by ignoring the behavior. Many dogs will stop if they don't receive ANY response on the part of the owners. This is easier said than done. If the dog persists after 15 minutes, calmly get up and with as little interaction as possible (no talking!), take the dog outside, go back and finish your meal. The dog will quickly learn that excessive barking will not be rewarded with attention or food. Although it can be a bit grating, most owners capable of ignoring barking for a week or so will see a marked decrease in the barking behavior. However, some dogs won't stop unless they are put outside. If the dog barks outside, ignore the behavior.

Remember, as with all problems, consistency, patience, and proper technique are essential. Do this and you will be successful.

STEALING FOOD FROM COUNTERS

This is a very common problem. Jumping on counters, especially to steal food, can be dangerous to your dog. There is no guarantee that the dog won't jump up on the counter and get uncooked chicken, lamb, pork or some sort of meat with bones that, if ingested, could cause medical problems. Additionally, most dogs will be far less inclined to want to eat their dog food if they've had the taste of forbidden fruits such as lasagna, ribs, T-bone steak or barbecued chicken. So it is best to teach the dog not to jump up on counters.

First, like every behavior, consistent training is critical to successfully modifying it. I have seen hundreds of dog owners standing by the counter preparing something to eat, then casually take a piece of food off the counter and hand it to the dog. When you do this, you teach your dog that food is on the counter. To be fair, most dogs suspect this anyway, since they can smell it. What many dog owners don't realize is that when you feed your dog from the counter, you are also teaching her that food *for dogs* is on the counter.

This problem can be handled by combining several training methods. First, don't feed the dog from the counter. Second, teach the dog that ignoring food on the counter is a good behavior and one you will reward. Third, learn the art of properly booby-trapping the counters to make sure the dog won't be able to get the food off the counter when she jumps up. Booby-trapping will teach the dog to associate negative consequences with jumping on the counters. Here is where punishment has a place in training. The simple fact is, dogs, like people, engage in behavior because that behavior is rewarding to them. In the case of stealing food off counters, the 12-ounce T-bone is a pretty good incentive to keep jumping. Especially after the dog gets the steak a few times.

Many owners and a few trainers try to solve the problem by correcting the dog when they see the behavior take place. That's fine as far as it goes, but the problem is most dogs will try a little counter thievery when you are not around. If they succeed, what do they learn? Answer: to grab the T-bone when you are not looking. Not exactly the lesson you want to teach.

Other trainers suggest strict management as the solution. By management, I mean *never* allowing the dog unsupervised accessibility to the counters, thus, preventing the behavior as opposed to correcting it. The problem here is that, especially when food is involved, dogs will be dogs and never is a very long time. Inevitably I get the call from a shocked owner whose 10-month-old dog ate a complete rib roast. "She's never done this before," they say. My question is usually, "Has she ever had the chance?" Often, the answer is "no." The bottom line is that management is an important tool in preventing this behavior, but it is not the only tool. I recommend a three-pronged approach (kind of like a fork) in dealing with this problem.

1. As I've already said, never ever feed the dog from the counters.

2. For at least four months, the dog should never have unsupervised access to the counters. This means a spot similar to the one you used when dining must be created for the dog. For the first two months, the dog should be in her spot if you are preparing food. During months three and four, periodically allow the dog to come by the counters when you are there preparing food. The dog should always be on a leash and head collar at these times. If the dog begins to jump on the counter, instantly say "no" and pull the dog away from the counter. Immediately put the dog back in her spot and don't give her another opportunity to engage in this behavior for at least a week.

   Consider whining, staring and begging (with pleading, starving eyes) to be unacceptable behaviors around the counters. If this occurs, swiftly say "no." If the dog stops after three seconds, briefly praise and go back to preparing the food. If the behavior occurs again, put her back in her spot. Additionally, make it a point to walk her by the counters on leash four or five times a day when food is out, consistently praising her for no jumping and no begging. If you do this consistently, you will find that after four months your dog ignores food on the counters—or does she?

3. After four months, give the dog an opportunity to steal food if she chooses. However, this opportunity will be a setup. This is where booby-trapping comes in.

    For example, put that T-bone on the counter and then booby-trap the counter with a motion-sensitive sound alarm. Let the dog in the kitchen and then walk out of the room. If the dog jumps up on the counter and attempts to grab the food, the alarm will sound. Remember to put the food far enough back on the counter so the dog can't get it. When the alarm sounds, get in there and tell the dog "no." Then immediately take the dog on leash over to the counter and praise her for not jumping. It is important the dog understand the behavior she is being corrected for is *jumping* on the counter, not walking near it.

    Some dogs will *not* be deterred by the sound of the alarm. For these dogs, I recommend the Radio Systems Scat Mat and a sound alarm. The Scat Mat is a flat plastic mat that emits a very low electrical charge when touched. It feels like a static shock and is not dangerous to pets or people. The mat should be placed on the counter with the food placed back far enough on the mat that the dog will not be able to reach the food without receiving several seconds' worth of this static shock. There is almost no dog who will do this to get the food.

    Additionally, the sound alarm will go off, which is your cue to get in there and tell the dog "no." Then, as noted above, immediately take the dog on leash over to the counter and praise her for not jumping.

Remember, consistency is extremely critical in shaping all behaviors, especially here, because any time the dog is able to jump up, get the food and get away with it, she is getting a very special reward for this behavior. That means access really must be prevented from areas where there might be food left out until the dog has been fully trained, specifically set up and tested.

JUMPING ON FURNITURE

Like stealing from the counters, jumping on furniture is a common problem. The solution is very similar to the counter-stealing challenge. This problem can be handled by combining three training methods: consistency, counterconditioning and correction.

1. First, consistency. The dog must not ever be allowed to jump on the furniture. It can't be OK some times but not others. This also means the dog cannot have unsupervised access to the furniture for a period of at least four months.

2. Second, counterconditioning. Start off teaching the dog to go to her spot whenever you are sitting on the furniture. This means making a spot that is comfortable and positive for the dog. Use a blanket or even a doggie bed and give your dog special treats or toys at the spot. For the first two months, the dog should be leashed to the spot to prevent her from wandering. Remember, make the spot comfortable and positive. This is where the dog goes *every time* you sit on the furniture. In addition to teaching the dog to associate positive things with being in her spot, it also teaches her to associate positive things with not jumping on the furniture.

3. During the third and fourth months, reinforce the idea that good things happen when she's not on the furniture by taking the dog over to the furniture on a leash and head collar and praising her when she walks by it without jumping. If she does jump, say "no" and gently guide her away using the leash. Then take her back to the furniture and praise her for not jumping. Do this specific exercise six or seven times every day for at least two months. I know it's a lot of work, but believe me, it's a lot less work than having to replace your furniture. After four months of consistent training, apply the art of booby-trapping just to make sure the dog really gets the lesson. Booby-trapping will teach the dog to associate negative things with jumping on furniture.

Starting at the beginning of month five, give the dog an opportunity to jump on the furniture if she chooses. However, this opportunity will be a setup. This is where booby-trapping comes in.

Most people have more than one piece of furniture in a room. It's not always practical to booby-trap each piece, so I recommend putting boxes on the furniture that's not booby-trapped during the setup. This way, the only piece of furniture the dog *can* jump on will be the booby-trapped one. You can always switch the boxes around and give the dog an opportunity to jump on different pieces of booby-trapped furniture on different days.

To properly booby-trap, set a motion-sensitive sound alarm near the furniture in a way that will trigger the alarm when the dog jumps up on it. This is an important point. The alarm should not be positioned so that it goes off when the dog goes near the furniture. You're looking to correct jumping on the furniture, not walking by it. Put your dog outside or in another part of the house and test the alarm yourself. Does it go off when you sit on the couch? If yes, it's probably set correctly.

When you're sure the alarm is set correctly, let the dog in and then walk out of the room. If the dog jumps up on the furniture, the alarm will sound loudly. When it does, get in there and tell the dog "no." Then immediately take the dog on leash over to the furniture and praise her for not jumping. This may sound strange, but it's important to show the dog the difference between jumping on the furniture, which is *bad*, and not jumping, which is *good*.

As I noted in the section on stealing food from the counter, some dogs will *not* be deterred by the sound of the alarm. For these dogs, I recommend the Radio Systems Scat Mat and a sound alarm. The Scat Mat is a flat plastic mat that emits a very low electrical charge when touched. It feels like a static shock and is not dangerous to pets or people. Place the mat on the furniture. When the dog jumps up, she will get a harmless but unpleasant zap. Dogs will look to avoid this zap by not jumping, much the way you'd avoid shaking someone's hand after walking across a shaggy carpet in loafers. Harmless, but unpleasant. Additionally, the sound alarm will go off, which is your cue to get in there and tell the dog "no." Then as I've already noted, immediately take the dog on leash over to the furniture and praise her for not jumping.

My own dog, the world's cutest Basset Hound, was a rescue whom I obtained at 10 months of age. This dog loved to be up on the couch. He had obviously learned this before I adopted him. Part of my solution was to get him his own bed. I then took him to this bed and proceeded to praise, feed, dance, laugh and generally make all his experiences on the bed very positive. This, coupled with a little creative booby-trapping, taught the dog in five months to stay off my couches. Five years later, he still doesn't go on them. He is so well trained that once, when I was on vacation, my pet sitter said she was concerned my dog might have a physical problem. I asked why and she said, "I spent three days trying to get him to jump up and sit with me on the couch. It's not that high a jump and he wouldn't even try. I thought maybe there was something wrong with his hips." I laughed and explained to her what a good boy he was. Everyone reading this book can have the same response from their dogs.

Many owners and a few dog trainers try to solve the furniture jumping problem by correcting the dog when they see the behavior take place. The problem with that is, most dogs will switch to jumping up when you are not around. If they succeed, they simply learn to take a nap on your chair when you're not there.

Other trainers suggest strict management as the solution. By management, I mean *never* allowing the dog unsupervised access to the furniture, thus, preventing the behavior as opposed to correcting it. Unlike the stealing food challenge, strict management might work in this case— but it might not. Booby-trapping will certainly let you know whether management did the trick. If you booby-trap the furniture and the dog never jumps up on it, then after a few months you can consider the problem solved. If management by itself didn't completely curb your dog's couch potato urges, I can assure you a few booby-trap experiences will.

Remember, consistency is extremely critical, as are patience and understanding.

EXCESSIVE BARKING

There are many reasons dogs bark and bark excessively. The word "excessively" is important, because a little barking is normal. Dogs bark to express themselves verbally, and they are entitled to a little verbal expression. However, barking that is triggered by the slightest provocation and/or goes on for more than a few seconds can be a problem.

Excessive barking is a tough problem to address in a book like this, because sometimes barking is a sign of aggressive behavior. This can be a very serious problem, as anyone facing a dominant 120-pound Rottweiler whose only desire is to make a meal of your leg can attest. Because of the risk, I am only going to cover the simpler and less dangerous types of barking in this book. If you have any suspicions that your dog may be aggressive, seek out a professional trainer for advice. I am a professional trainer, but a local pro will need to come out and observe you, your family and your dog to get the specific information needed to make a proper diagnosis and assist you.

That said, to address any barking problem, it is important to first know why your dog is barking because solutions vary based on what is motivating the dog to bark. Let's look at three types of barking and ways to address them:

1. Excited play alert barking

2. Learned barking

3. Boredom barking

Excited Play Alert Barking

This barking is usually directed at things the dog sees but can't get to. These things may include other dogs, people, a ball, squirrels or other small animals such as cats. Most puppies begin exhibiting this type of barking by four and half months of age.

The barking dog's demeanor is playful and excited. Look at the dog's body language. Body posture often includes play bowing or bouncing around. Play bowing is when the dog puts her head toward the ground and sticks her bottom in the air. It's a cute, wiggly, bouncy kind of posture—the dog looks like she's playing. You do not have to be an expert to recognize this. Facial features are generally relaxed, with ears held loose. Her tail may be wagging, but not stiffly. The hackles on her back are not up. While she's bouncing around, she's also barking. It is cute, but after a while the barking can be a little difficult to endure. Neighbors may agree.

To deal with this type of barking, you need to take a couple of steps. First, most dogs won't bark unless they become *really* excited. So, for a period of three or four months, try to avoid deliberately getting your dog so wound up that she spends the next 20 minutes barking and bouncing around. This doesn't mean you can't play with the dog. It simply means don't get her completely worked up. When playing, if she does become overly excited, stop the game for a few minutes until she calms down and stops barking.

The dog should also learn to engage in an alternative behavior when confronted with the types of things that stimulate this barking. For example, if she really gets excited, refocus her attention on a favorite toy.

It is really critical to focus on teaching your dog to listen to you, first without distractions and then with distractions. Teaching her to listen to you around the types of things that may stimulate her barking will be very helpful in enabling you to attain enough control to eliminate this behavior. Remember to enthusiastically praise acceptable nonbarking focused behavior whenever it occurs, especially around distractions. If a dog barks when she sees squirrels and her owner patiently and persistently works the dog in obedience exercises while around squirrels, praising all nonbarking behavior, over time this dog will learn to watch her owner and not bark, even around squirrels.

This type of motivational technique is desirable when working with excited play alert barking. Physically punishing a dog for play alert barking may initially suppress the barking, but you run the risk of the dog developing negative associations to whatever she was barking at, increasing the likelihood of a future aggression problem. That being said, I will go on record that sometimes it may be necessary to administer a correction for excessive play barking. The correction should only be administered after a "quiet" command (so it is really a correction for not following your command), and should always be followed by rewards such as praise, petting, food treats and toys once the dog is silent for at least two seconds. These rewards for silence after a correction are important to prevent the dog from developing negative associations with the thing she was barking at. A dog who barks at children riding bicycles may begin to dislike children if she associates corrections with children.

Corrections may include a gentle yank on the leash and head collar. The most important criteria for choosing a correction is that it must be effective in just one or two applications and it must not stress or frighten the dog, only stop the barking. Using a gentle yank on the leash as an example, a complete training scenario might sound like this:

After three months of teaching his dog to listen and focus when there is little or nothing going on around them, Mr. Smith takes his dog to a quiet street where squirrels are frequently seen both on the ground and in the trees. Mr. Smith's dog, a seven-month-old Labrador Retriever puppy named Cole, loves squirrels and would happily spend his life barking at them. Mr. Smith works Cole for a few minutes to get his focus before going to the squirrel street. Once there, Cole sees the squirrels and starts barking. Mr. Smith tells Cole "quiet," waits two long seconds, and when Cole does not respond he gently tugs Cole's leash, causing Cole to focus on Mr. Smith. The head collar is very effective for this type of training. Mr. Smith does not hurt Cole, and his objective when tugging the leash is not to cause pain, but to temporarily shift Cole's focus from the squirrels to him. After Cole looks at Mr. Smith for two seconds, Mr. Smith praises and rewards Cole for his nonbarking, focused behavior. This keeps Cole focused on his owner for an additional 10 seconds, before Cole forgets himself and starts barking at the squirrels again. When this occurs, Mr. Smith repeats the entire sequence. Mr. Smith does this at least three times a week for two to four months. If he keeps it up, he will be able to take Cole anywhere without excessive barking.

While this behavior can take a while to control, it is certainly workable. Other things worth mentioning: If you encourage your dog to chase cats or any small animals, stop now. You should also be careful not to praise your dog in an attempt to calm her down. The only time praise should be given is when the dog is not barking.

Learned Barking

Generally if a behavior is successful, it will likely occur again. In most cases of excessive barking, there will be some learned behavior regardless of whether the initial motivation for barking was excited play barking, boredom or something else. The most common examples of learned barking include barking at the owner or other people for attention, barking at the door to be let in or out, barking at a ball or toy so the owner will throw it, and barking at an owner or a cabinet for food. Often, owners will reward the exact behavior they wish to prevent. For example, the dog barks to be let in or out and you let the dog in or out. The dog barks to be petted and you pet the dog. You're by the cabinet that contains the dog treats when your dog barks and you say something like, "She's so smart. She knows where the food is," and then give the dog a treat. In situations like these, it's easy to see why some dogs learn to bark: It gets them what they want.

Sometimes not just dog owners, but also family and friends reward unacceptable barking behavior. This further stimulates the barking problem. To eliminate this type of behavior, several things need to happen.

First, owners must identify all circumstances in which the dog barks and honestly assess whether they or others are rewarding the barking. Once you've identified how and when you're encouraging the dog to bark, stop rewarding this behavior.

Two, immediately start an obedience program with your dog. The goal is to get your dog to obey basic commands such as sit, sit-stay, come, down, down-stay, loose leash walking or heeling without distractions, and eventually around distractions. This can take four to six months, sometimes even longer. It is critical for success. Also included in the list of basic commands is no.

Three, look to teach alternative appropriate behaviors (instead of barking) that the dog can be rewarded for. This will not always be possible, but certainly it can be accomplished in most cases. For example, if your dog barks to be let in or out, consider installing a doggie door or consider teaching the dog to come and lie at your feet whenever she has to go out. This is not as difficult as it sounds. Of course, the dog needs to know how to come and lie down, which is why obedience is so important.

Assuming your dog understands these commands, how would you teach a dog to come and lie down, as opposed to barking, when she has to go outside? The answer: Every time she barks to be let out, tell her "no." If necessary, consistently put her on a leash and head collar. This way you can give her a gentle tug if the "no" isn't enough to stop her from barking. The instant she is quiet, tell her "good girl" and then have her come and lie down by you. As soon as she does this, praise and take her outside. Do this every single time she has to go out. After three or four months, she will run over to you and lie down when she has to go outside.

This is admittedly a little tougher to teach when she has to come inside. For that challenge, you will need to think of another acceptable behavior. Some dogs scratch on the door with their paw or even ring a little bell. Others simply sit quietly by the door. Whatever behavior you choose, the key is to reward the behavior by letting her in. Also, do not allow anyone else to reward your dog for any type of learned barking.

A word of caution regarding ignoring undesirable behavior. Owners must be prepared for an initial increase in barking. The behavior got the desired reaction in the past, so the dog will just turn it up to try to get what she wants now. Behaviorists call this an *extinction burst,* but I have always just called it irritating. Bottom line, consistency is critical, so is patience, understanding, and maybe a little more patience.

Boredom Barking

Some breeds of dogs are more inclined to whine, bark or howl when they are bored. If your dog is barking, howling or whining and a cause cannot be determined, start by taking her to a veterinarian. Sometimes dogs vocalize when they are in pain. Often there may be no external signs of the pain, such as when dogs are suffering from dental disease, urinary tract infections, ear infections and other conditions.

Boredom barking can go on for hours. Solutions include giving the dog more mental and physical stimulation. Since dogs are social animals, obtaining another dog for company or employing a dog walker can be helpful. A proper exercise program and toys such as chew toys, Buster Cubes and other interactive toys, and hunting for hidden food treats are all effective remedies. Corrections are somewhat difficult, since this type of behavior often occurs when no one is around. Sometimes a recording of your and your family's voices may be played for additional stimulation.

As I've already mentioned, barking needs to be dealt with cautiously because it is often a precursor to aggressive behavior. Owners are advised to be careful and take the time to properly identify why their dog is barking before attempting to treat it. If you are unsure, contact a professional. As with all problems, owners need to remember that solutions do not occur overnight and that practice, patience and consistency are the formula for good results.

CHAPTER 6

SIMPLE, EFFECTIVE WAYS TO ADDRESS BASIC PROBLEMS, PART 2

In this chapter we're going to work on more behavior problems. Your goals in this chapter are the same as they were in Chapter 5:

1. Identify the problem you wish to address.
2. Learn the solutions to the behavior problem you wish to solve.
3. Apply the solution with patience, consistency, understanding and love.

Now let's address three more behavioral challenges:

1. Chewing
2. Housebreaking
3. Digging

CHEWING

Chewing is among the most common problems I see as a dog trainer. As with all problems, it is important to understand why your dog does what he does. When it comes to chewing, the answer is really quite basic: Chewing is a very natural behavior for dogs. Many dogs chew because they are bored. They chew because they are teething. Sometimes they chew because of separation anxiety or because they have been given inappropriate items to chew on by their owners. Dogs chew due to inadequate or improper diet and finally, they chew because they like to.

Remember, dogs are intelligent and are especially inquisitive when they're puppies. Plus, they do not have hands. This is an important point. Think about how often a one- or two-year-old child exploring his new environment touches things. Since the dog does not have hands, when he explores he will taste and chew. This is very normal behavior.

The bottom line on chewing is that you are not going to stop your dog from chewing.

It is just not reasonable or realistic to expect otherwise. So, if you can't eliminate this problem, what can you do? The answer is to redirect it. In this chapter you will learn how to teach your dog to chew on the proper things, as opposed to improper items like your furniture, clothing, etc.

The real key to addressing problem chewing is to strongly fixate your dog on chewing the correct items. If you can get your dog to chew on the proper items 70 percent more than he does right now, then your dog is going to chew 70 percent less on the improper items. That, coupled with things like proper exercise, proper diet and making some of the unacceptable items less available, as well as teaching your dog what not to chew, is how we'll address this problem.

Remember, most dogs chew. This actually makes the problem easier to deal with. Why? Because the chewing behavior is such a strong, instinctive behavior, it will be fairly simple to fixate your dog on the correct items. While you are teaching your dog to fixate on the correct items, you must prevent him from chewing inappropriate objects at all times, whether you are around or not.

Let's talk first about fixating your dog on the correct items. I recommend hard plastic bones, such as Nylabones, or hard rubber toys like Kongs and Rhinos. These products are excellent examples of proper chew toys.

I would stay away from chew toy products that are similar to the types of your things you don't want your dog to chew on. For example, if your dog chews your carpeting, pants or couch cushions, it is wise to stay away from fabric chew toys. Additionally, toys with moving parts or pieces that can be broken off and accidentally ingested may pose a risk to your pet. Let's keep it simple and safe.

Some trainers recommend real bones, such as marrowbones. I have found that while most dogs love these items, the bones can often leave a scent on floors, especially carpeting. This is a problem when the bones are not around and the delicious meat-scented carpeting is. I've seen dogs chew up entire carpeted rooms, so I'd be very careful. Some real bones are sterilized and sold just for dogs. They have been treated so that no meat or grease remains. This eliminates the scent challenge, but such bones, in my opinion, are about as appealing as rocks.

Not every dog likes Nylabones, although most can be taught to if you follow these instructions. Take your dog's Nylabone and soak it for 15 minutes every day in chicken or beef broth. Then make sure that whenever you play with your dog, you make the bone a primary source of interaction between you and your pet. If you play the two-toy game mentioned on page 75, use the bone. When you greet your dog, it should be with bone in hand. When you depart, give your dog the bone. Pet your dog with the bone. Touch the bone. Act coy with the bone. Let your dog see you "hide" the bone in an accessible location and then encourage your dog to find it.

Most owners who really take this to heart find that their dogs very quickly focus on their chew bones. They also find that when their dogs chew far more on the correct items, they chew far less on the wrong items.

I would also get at least half a dozen of these bones, leave two or three available to the dog for a week, and then switch them with the other three. You can leave the bones that are not in use in a container of broth in the refrigerator. Nylabones are safe and they work. So do Kong and Rhino toys, which are hollow. These items can be made even more appealing by putting a little cheese or peanut butter and honey in the center of the toy. Most dogs will spend hours trying to lick and chew these tasty items out of the center.

When you see your dog chewing on his toys, definitely let him know you are pleased: "Good boy." Speak in light, easy, calm tones, so as not to distract the dog and stop him from chewing on the items that you want him to chew on.

During the first four months of training your dog to not chew inappropriately, prevent the dog from having *any* unsupervised access to inappropriate items. This means you must watch the dog at all times when he's in the house so that you can stop any unacceptable chewing immediately. This means keeping your dog on a leash and head collar when he is in the house. He can walk around dragging the leash. *(Never leave your dog unattended on a leash and head collar.)* Additionally, if your dog has a chewing problem, he might chew a leather or nylon leash. Consider a chain link leash.

Putting the dog on a leash can save owners a lot of problems. Unleashed dogs can often take inappropriate items and not want to give them back. If your dog grabs something you don't want him to have, chasing him all over the house simply shows the dog that this is an excellent way to get your attention. It also teaches him that, more often than not, running away will result in the dog's victory, since you are going to be hard-pressed to catch the dog when he runs away. Avoid this trap by leashing the dog during the training process.

Before you let your dog in the house, remove all the inappropriate chewing items you find. I am not suggesting that you remove your couches. However, I would definitely pick up shoes, articles of clothing, tissue paper, the paperback book left on the floor, the kid's toys, etc. The fewer opportunities that present themselves, the easier it will be to fixate your dog on the correct items.

That being said, some dogs just *have to* chew certain things. They may be items you couldn't remove or things you missed. When you see your dog chewing an inappropriate object, quickly say "no" and gently pull your dog by the leash away from the object he's chewing. Immediately give him the appropriate toy, and when he starts chewing on it for roughly two seconds, praise this behavior.

If your dog continues to return to specific inappropriate items, for example, a tasty table leg or couch cushion, consider a chew repellent such as Bitter Apple. Products like Bitter Apple are designed to taste horrible. When it is lightly sprayed on inappropriate items, your dog will experience the tasty table leg in a very different way. It will taste awful. This, coupled with you saying "no," pulling the dog away and then giving the dog a proper, yummy toy, is a very effective way of communicating what is and isn't acceptable for chewing. Most chew repellents tend to evaporate fairly quickly. This means you will probably need to reapply them once or twice a day. Also, always test any repellent on a small area to make sure it doesn't stain or damage your property. Finally (and I spoke about this in the section on nipping in Chapter 5), consider spraying the Bitter Apple directly into the dog's mouth the *first* time you have to use it. I need everyone to be clear about this: What I'm saying is, the very first time you *ever* use Bitter Apple for anything is the only time you should spray it in your pet's mouth. It sounds mean, but it isn't. And it will most assuredly teach the dog to have a very negative association with the taste of Bitter Apple.

Some owners must leave their dogs in areas (such as the house) where the dog can chew when they're not around. If you fall into this category, I strongly recommend that you consider crating your dog during the training process. By *crating* I mean giving your dog a place where he can't get into trouble when you're gone. Several companies manufacture dog crates that can be used for this purpose. As I have already explained, crating is not cruel and it is not recommended as a correction or punishment. Crating is a form of what trainers call *management,* and it works. Throughout this book, I have spoken about consistency. Chewing is no exception. Please consider it this way: If your dog chews 120 times per day and pretty much every one of these times it's on the correct items, or you're present to redirect your dog when he chews on the wrong stuff, you're going to eliminate the chewing problem. If your dog chews 120 times per day and 30 or 40 of these times it's on inappropriate items, solving this problem will be far more difficult. The problem can be even tougher to solve if your dog has numerous positive experiences chewing on the wrong stuff. This is why management coupled with strong fixation on correct items is the only real way many owners get a handle on the chewing challenge. Some owners can safely leave their dogs in a yard or have a dog run constructed for management. However you deal with it, the key in management is controlling the environment.

After awhile, you will slowly be able to give your dog unsupervised access to your home. But this does take time. I would spend at least four months restricting access while you focus the dog on the correct items, and when he no longer attempts to chew inappropriate things in front of you, start to give him very limited amounts of unsupervised access.

Many owners resist the idea of management. In my opinion, leaving an untrained dog loose in the house all day is like leaving an average two-year-old unattended in a house full of breakable objects for hours at a time.

Proper diet must be considered when addressing a chewing problem. A high-quality premium hard kibble is important to make sure the dog isn't chewing due to nutritional deficiencies. The dog will get a lot of chewing satisfaction from eating the kibble. After all, it is unlikely that you or I would be satisfied with a mushy diet, because we would want to sink our teeth into something hard or crunchy. It's the same with dogs who are fed a strictly soft food diet. Also, check with your veterinarian regarding vitamin supplements. I have seen dogs who chewed tens of thousands of dollars worth of furniture cease all chewing when they were put on a high-quality diet. Proper nutrition must not be overlooked when addressing a chewing problem.

The same thing goes for exercise. It is vitally important for your dog's health that he get adequate exercise. Obviously, "adequate" will differ from breed to breed and dog to dog, but dogs who get a good deal of exercise chew far less than dogs who get little or none. To start an exercise program, check with your vet to make sure your dog is in good health and get exercise suggestions based on your dog's specific condition. On a personal note, I have a Basset Hound, which is not known as the world's most active breed. I take my dog for a two-mile walk at least four times a week. This works for us, and my dog has remained lean (for a Basset) and in excellent condition.

Remember, the solution to this problem is not to spray your house with a chew repellent, nor is it to crate your dog. The solution is a combination of all the things I've mentioned: strong fixation on the correct items, management, teaching the dog what inappropriate items are, proper diet and exercise.

As I have said in my discussions of all these problems, chewing will only be effectively addressed if you understand that it will require patience, consistency and proper application of the solutions I've outlined.

HOUSEBREAKING

Housebreaking is one of the more common problems dog owners face. The basic principles of housebreaking are relatively simple, although applying those principles to your individual circumstances can sometimes be a little tricky.

Let's start off with some simple solutions, so I can help some owners right away.

Does your dog only have accidents at night? By accidents, I mean the dog goes to the bathroom in the house. Night is defined as from when you go to bed until when you wake up. If the answer is yes, try the following suggestions.

The dog should not be permitted any food or water at least two hours before bedtime. Additionally, take the dog out for his final walk and elimination as late as you possibly can. Often, this is all that's needed.

If your dog is going to the bathroom in the house more frequently and clearly doesn't understand where he should eliminate, you will need to put him on a proper housebreaking schedule. For most people, crating the dog is the most effective way to housetrain. The crate should be small enough that your dog can stand up and turn around, lie down and comfortably stretch out, but no larger than that.

Crate training works because most dogs do not like to eliminate where they have to lie. This is sometimes misunderstood by owners, who think their dog won't eliminate where he sleeps and eats. A dog would happily eliminate in a large bedroom, even if he slept there. He will also eliminate in his crate, if the crate is large enough for him to still lie down in a clean spot. If the dog is confined to the right size crate, he will probably not eliminate in it. This is extremely important information. If you can prevent the dog from eliminating, you can then take the dog out to where you want him to go, with a much greater likelihood that he will do so.

Fifty percent of housebreaking involves positively reinforcing the correct behavior—that is, praising the dog when he eliminates in the proper place. The other 50 percent is management, so you can prevent the dog from going in the wrong place until you can take him out to eliminate in the right one.

The basic scenario for housebreaking goes like this: Confine your dog. After a few hours, take the dog from the crate to the location you want him to eliminate in. Remember to take the dog out the same door to the same location every time you want him to eliminate. Wait 10 minutes for him to do so. If he goes within the 10 minutes, praise, reward (a small treat) and wait an extra two or three minutes to make

A typical crate. It should be large enough for your dog to lie down and be comfortable.

certain he's done everything he has to do. Then take him back in the house and give him 20 to 30 minutes of supervised "free time." Use a timer and be very strict about not allowing the dog more than 20 or 30 minutes of freedom. When the timer goes off, you have a choice. You may take the dog back out to eliminate again, and if he goes, repeat the process of praise and free time; or you can confine the dog again.

Mistakes are made when owners give their dogs too much free time, fail to take the dog out again, fail to reconfine the dog when the time is up, or fail to wait the extra two to three minutes after he eliminates the first time.

If you take your dog out and the dog fails to eliminate within 10 minutes, he should also be confined again. It is important to understand that this confinement is not punishment. It is simply a way of preventing the dog from going to the bathroom in the wrong place.

Consistent feeding and watering schedules are also vital to your housebreaking efforts. Dogs should be fed at fixed times and given no more than 10 to 15 minutes in which to eat. Free feeding—leaving food available for your dog to eat all the time—is not recommended when you are housebreaking your dog. Water may be given during free time and when you take the dog to eliminate. It can also be given sparingly when the dog is being confined (although not for two hours before bedtime or at night). The reason feeding and watering schedules are so important is that free access to food and water will make it almost impossible to predict when your dog will have to eliminate. It will also make it far more likely that your dog will eliminate in the crate. By controlling when your dog eats and drinks, you make housebreaking much simpler.

Please note that young puppies may find it very difficult to avoid eliminating for longer than three to six hours. A good guide is to add an hour for every month of a puppy's life. That is, a three-month-old puppy can hold it for three hours, a four-month-old for four hours, and so on. Be careful about allowing the dog water during these long periods. Also, never confine the dog in direct sun or for longer than eight hours.

If your dog eliminates in the crate, you may have confined him too long or the crate may be too big. Remember, the crate should be large enough for your dog to comfortably lie in, but not so huge that he can walk all the way to the other side and be well out of the way of any mess he made. If you are unclear, contact a local professional trainer.

If the dog has an accident in the house, correction after the fact is not only a waste of time, but is counterproductive. Correcting your dog after the fact just confuses the dog.

Instead, ask yourself what you could have done differently to prevent the behavior. Did you give the dog too much freedom? When the dog eliminated outside, did you give the dog an extra three minutes to make sure he did what he had to do? Does he have unlimited access to food and water? Generally, your dog will need to eliminate outside consistently with no accidents in the house for two to three weeks before he understands that outside is the only place he should eliminate. Please remember that some dogs will take longer to housetrain than others.

Once your dog learns it, you can increase the amount of free time the dog gets. For example, instead of 20 to 30 minutes of free time, increase it to 40 to 60 minutes. After a few more weeks, you can increase the time even more. Consider, whenever possible, a dog door, because it makes housebreaking much easier in most cases.

Paper training is generally not recommended, except when the dog cannot be given access to the outside for periods greater than eight

COURTESY ABSORPTION CORP.

A housebreaking student in a Puppy Go Potty (PGP) tray with absorbent "litter."

*An exercise pen with two
housebreaking students.*

hours at a time, or in areas where it is unsafe, too cold, hot, etc. If this is your situation, consider a potty training kit such as Puppy Go Potty. These kits contain absorbent paper "litter" and a waterproof tray. The materials are similar to a cat litter box and are much cleaner than using old newspaper.

To train your dog to use the box, you will also need a puppy exercise pen. This is a metal collapsible pen that you can put on the ground or floor and place your dog in. The pen can be expanded to form a circle approximately six feet in diameter. (If you have a small dog, make the exercise pen smaller than six feet.) Place the waterproof PGP tray on one side of the circle. This is where the dog needs to be when you are not there to supervise him. When the dog can no longer control his bodily functions, he will most likely defecate and urinate in the tray. When you are home, the housebreaking procedures I have already outlined should be followed.

Avoid dietary changes during the housebreaking process. If such changes are unavoidable, try to switch the dog gradually to the new food, to avoid stomach upsets. (Diarrhea makes it extremely difficult to housebreak. If your dog gets diarrhea, you should immediately call your veterinarian.) A good general formula is to feed two-thirds old food to one-third new food the first week, two-thirds new food to one-third old food the second week and completely new food the third week.

Housebreaking can be a bit tedious, but it is not complicated, provided you are consistent as well as patient.

DIGGING

Like all the other problems I've addressed, digging is a common and very normal behavior for dogs. As with all problems, it is important to understand the reasons behind the behavior. With digging there are many motives. Dogs dig because they are bored. They dig when it is hot because they like to lie in holes to get cooler. They dig to escape. They bury objects. Sometimes dogs simply dig because they like to.

In dealing with a digging problem, first understand that every dog has a certain amount of energy to expend each day. Sufficient exercise is often an excellent way to burn off excess energy and frequently helps in curtailing digging behavior. In two decades, I have seen dogs who literally destroyed entire yards. I worked with a Saint Bernard who actually uprooted 15-foot trees. This dog, and many others, stopped digging when they were put on a reasonable, consistent exercise program. Remember, exercise programs will vary from breed to breed and dog to dog, so check with your veterinarian. Also remember that simply leaving your dog alone in the yard does not count as exercise. *You* must exercise the dog.

Boredom is a common reason for dogs to dig. If you leave the dog first thing in the morning without a lot to keep him occupied, he is going to have to do *something* to keep himself busy. One of the things dogs often do to occupy themselves is dig. To counter this, you need to give your dog things to do that are more interesting to him than digging holes.

Luckily, there are a number of creative toys that can keep most dogs occupied and interested. Consider toys like a Buster Cube or

Boomer Ball. The Buster Cube is a plastic square that you can put small pieces of food in. The dog can get the food, but only after shaking and moving the cube around. This will keep many dogs focused for hours. Boomer Balls are hard plastic balls that some dogs love to chase around. They are generally too large for most dogs to fit in their mouths, although many dogs will certainly try. Some dogs will bat at the ball with their paws, push it around the yard with their chests and have a great time playing ball and not digging holes.

Make it a point to play with your dog and these toys in the yard. Doing this will get the dog interested in the toys and teach him there are other fun activities in the yard besides digging. Nylabones, Kongs, and Rhino toys will also focus your dog on something other than digging.

Aside from giving your dog sufficient exercise and interesting things to do in the yard, make sure your dog is on a high-quality premium hard kibble. Stay away from foods that are often loaded with hidden sugars, chemicals and preservatives (hidden sugars in the form of beet pulp, sucrose, fructose, etc., can exacerbate the dog's energy levels and lead to digging), such as semi-moist dog foods.

If your dog considers the backyard (or wherever he digs) to be a place of banishment, it is more likely digging will occur there. I am not suggesting that you leave your dog in the house if you do not feel the dog is trustworthy. I am suggesting that your dog should think of the backyard as more than just a place of banishment. Most owners don't want their dogs to feel this way and are unaware of why the dog does. Stop and think about it. Are you like millions of people who put your dog out in the backyard every day you go to work? Many dogs will feel a certain level of anxiety if the backyard is the place where they're always left alone. For many owners, this can't be helped. I understand this, and all I'm suggesting is that you give your dog other, more positive experiences in the yard, as well. For example, play with the dog in the backyard regularly. You can also feed the dog in the backyard and obedience train your dog in the backyard. Help the dog to associate positive things with the yard and you will be eliminating one of the major causes of digging.

Make sure your dog has fun experiences in the yard. Steve demonstrates that neither he nor his student believe in all work.

When it comes to digging cooling holes, this is something that is a little tough to eliminate. There are parts of the country where it gets hot, sometimes all year round. There are specific breeds of dogs—longhaired breeds especially—who are going to need a place to be cool during the heat of the day.

There are several things you can try here, including providing some sort of overhang the dog can lie under for shade. You might consider a well-ventilated doghouse where the dog can get out of the heat of the sun. You might also consider having a small wading pool—the little plastic pools that you might buy for a young child—for your dog to lie in. I have seen dogs who were content to lie in one or two inches of water in a pool, and although they were muddy at the end of the day, they were far less motivated to dig because they were able to get cool. Hoses that throw up a fine mist are available at hardware stores. They are not only good for cooling, but can keep flies away. Finally, keep your longhaired dogs' hair cut short during the hotter months. These are definitely things worth trying if you are dealing with a digging dog in a hot climate.

Some dogs will bury bones or other objects and then dig them up later. This can sometimes present a challenge when you are dealing with a bored dog, since one of the ways to address the issue of boredom, aside from exercise, is to give the dog appropriate or alternative things to keep him occupied during the day. The problem is that if you give your dog a number of toys and he is inclined to bury these toys, you may be encouraging the digging behavior. There are ways around this. This can include making sure the dog has bigger toys, especially the Boomer Ball, which is larger than what most dogs will attempt to bury. If you are giving your dog smaller toys to play with, you can consider either drilling a hole in the toy or, in the case of say, the Nylabone, passing a wire through the bone and tying it to a tree or to the fence. This may sound a bit crazy, but it can prevent the dog from burying the toy, since it is now tied to something. Unfortunately, this method won't work with Buster Cubes.

As unpleasant as it may sound, a tried-and-true method to help cut down on digging is to bury the dog's fecal matter in the holes he has already dug. Many dogs will go back and dig in the same spot, and seem to find the act of digging in poop unpleasant.

Do not let your dog see you digging. If you are planting a flower bed, filling in holes your dog has dug or laying in a sprinkler system, make sure you put the dog somewhere else. Your dog will not understand why it's OK for you to dig in the garden, but not him.

Digging is a behavior that, more often than not, will occur when you are not around. It is important to understand that this is not because the dog is being sneaky or attempting to get away with something. It happens because when you are there, you provide the type of stimulus necessary to prevent the dog from digging. Most digging happens because of boredom. *If you cannot catch the dog in the act of digging, correction after the fact is not only a waste of time, but is often counterproductive.* Coming home, taking the dog over to a hole and chastising him in any way will, at best, teach the dog to dread your coming home and can foster anxiety. It will not eliminate the digging.

You can also play a game called "hunting for hidden treats." I have had great success with taking pieces of kibble, dog biscuits and/or some of the toys that I mentioned earlier and hiding them in various places in the backyard. I then encourage the dog to find these items.

Remember to praise your dog's appropriate
behaviors. Training should be positive.

Once you have taught the dog to do this, you can hide these things just before you leave the dog alone in the yard, let him outside, and send him on his treasure hunt. This will give the dog something to keep him occupied during the day. Please don't hide the toys by burying them!

One of the things people don't do often enough is focus on praising their dog's appropriate behaviors, because they are too busy looking for ways to correct inappropriate ones. This is very important in digging. When you see your dog out in the backyard, doing the right thing, praise that behavior. Remember, the more you positively reinforce a behavior, the stronger that behavior is going to be and the greater the likelihood that the dog will engage in it—both when you are there and when you are not.

Remember that certain dogs have been bred to dig. Terriers and Dachshunds come to mind. Dachshunds were bred to hunt badgers by following them into their burrows. They have a very strong predisposition to dig, and you may find that dogs so predisposed may not be stopped from digging. When dealing with these types of dogs, it might be necessary to teach your dog to dig in one spot. This may sound strange, but the principle is similar to that used to address chewing. In other words, accept the fact that your dog will dig and teach your dog to dig in one spot. The more he digs there, the less he will dig elsewhere.

This can be accomplished by teaching your dog to dig in a baited digging pit. Set up a digging pit where the ground is relatively soft, then bury items that you know the dog is likely to want to dig up: special food treats, toys, and so on. You can also let the dog see you digging there, and even take the dog over and encourage the dog to dig in this area. Praise him when he digs in the appropriate spot. Most dogs will grasp the concept very quickly. This, coupled with burying their dog's fecal matter in holes outside the digging pit, enable many owners to control and live with digging dogs.

Escape is yet another reason dogs dig. This type of digging can be more complex to deal with, because often the digging is a sign of an underlying problem. For example, a dog who is not being taught to behave appropriately around people, who is jumping up and acting unruly, might be ignored by an owner who finds the behavior unacceptable but doesn't take the time to teach the dog proper skills. Dogs are social, and if they have little or no contact with you, this can create anxiety that can lead to behaviors such as escape digging.

Un-neutered male dogs might try to dig out of the yard to roam your neighborhood, especially if they smell a female in heat.

To deal with escape behavior, first try to figure out why your dog is digging and then find the solution to that problem in this book. If you can't find it here, seek the assistance of a professional trainer.

In closing, it is important to remember that digging is a very normal behavior in dogs and is not the kind of behavior that is typically going to be eliminated overnight. In many instances digging is not going to be completely eliminated at all, although it can certainly be controlled and curtailed. Be optimistic, but also be realistic when dealing with a digging problem. As with all problems, make sure you understand that patience and consistency are the keys to success.

CHAPTER 7

Off-Leash Obedience

As I noted in Chapter 2, most people need their dog to be obedient off leash. I am not suggesting that owners violate local leash laws and take their dog for a jaunt down a public street off leash. What I am saying is that at the very least your dog needs to respond to simple commands such as "come," "sit," "stay" and "down" in the house and yard, and around distractions, without a leash. Believe me, it can be a lifesaver for your dog to consistently respond to these commands.

In Chapter 2 I also discussed why it's so difficult for people to get a dependable off-leash response from their dogs. Part of the reason is that for many years, most training techniques were based on punishment and involved using a leash and some sort of collar as a correction tool. Dogs were taught to avoid being yanked, and while this type of training sometimes generates decent control on leash, when the leash is removed the dog realizes your ability to inflict punishment on her no longer exists. At that point, the dog often does not comply. Today, modern training methods are based on reward rather than punishment, thus eliminating that focus on punishment tools—such as the leash.

The other reason owners have found attaining off-leash control to be so difficult is that some dog owners inadvertently teach their dogs not to respond to them off leash. This happens when owners give hundreds, and sometimes thousands, of off-leash commands from the first day they bring their dogs home, without any reinforcement at all. If you are unclear about why this creates problems in getting an off-leash response, please go back to Chapter 2.

The focus here will be to teach you an effective way to establish off-leash control of your dog *before* you start on-leash training. In point of fact, if this is done correctly, the leash and training collar will probably not even be used to teach "sit," "stay," "come" and "down." Instead, it will be used as a safety measure (just in case) when you take your dog around difficult distractions, such as other dogs, cats, people, public places and so on. Of course, it should also be used to teach loose leash walking and/or heel, which I will not cover in this book.

Owners who successfully train their dogs to consistently respond to the "sit," "stay," "come" and "down" commands off leash with distractions around the house and yard will have what I call *foundation level obedience*. Please understand that foundation level obedience does not mean your dog is completely trained. To attain that, you will need to work your dog on these obedience commands around numerous distractions in a public place, on leash. This should begin in a professionally run group obedience class. For instructions on how to find a good trainer and what to look for in an obedience class, please read Chapter 8.

FOUNDATION LEVEL OBEDIENCE

The most important command you will ever teach your dog is "come." If your dog comes on command, regardless of distractions or circumstances, you will be able to take her to an almost unlimited number of places. Imagine allowing your dog to run across a field, on a deserted beach, ahead of you as you hike on a mountain trail. Do you care if she's 100 or 200 feet ahead? Not if you know she will come every time you call! Is this really possible? Yes, but it's not easy and it doesn't happen overnight. It will take you many, many months, possibly years.

The first rule in teaching "come" is to become aware of how many times you tell your dog to come without enforcing it. Remember, any time you tell your dog to come (or anything else) and don't follow through with some form of reinforcement, at best you are teaching your dog not to listen on the first command, and at worst not to listen at all. This sabotages your obedience training and must stop immediately.

I'm going to assume that anyone reading this chapter needs to teach their dog to come consistently off leash on the first command around distractions, so I want you all to please stop giving the "come" command under any circumstances other than the ones listed in this chapter.

Inevitably, when I give suggestions like this to students in my classes, a dialogue something like this ensues:

Student: "OK, I understand. So tell me, Steve, what do I do when my dog has grabbed my sock and is running across the room? Are you saying I can't tell him to come? What about if he's running out the door? Or about to get into something? Can I call him then?"

Steve: "No. Telling him to come doesn't work, as evidenced by the fact that you're here to teach him to come. All you're doing is reinforcing that he doesn't have to come."

Student: "So, what do I do when he's stealing things, running out the door or getting into something?"

Steve: "If he's stealing things, he needs to be more strongly focused on chewing the correct objects and better managed by being kept on a leash when he's around you in the house. If he does get something, you can certainly call his name, but I would not give the 'c' command, because we've already established that he won't listen to it. Running out the door is also a management and prevention issue and not something that you will stop, at this point, by giving him the 'come' command. The bottom line is, at the level your dog is at right now, giving the 'come' command is counterproductive to training."

Student: "Then how do we teach our dogs to come?"

Steve: "I'm glad you asked."

COME

Before I go any further, a word about puppies and adult dogs. These exercises will work best with puppies under the age of four months. There are a number of reasons for this. First, puppies under four months are usually more inclined to follow and come to you, especially if you squat down. Second, younger puppies haven't had as much training not to listen. That being said, owners with dogs from four months to 15 years have shown dramatic training progress using these methods.

Can you teach an old dog new tricks? Yes, but it takes longer. Actually, it's not so much about the age of the dog as it is about the age of the behavior. Unfortunately, the older the dog, the greater the likelihood that an unacceptable behavior, such as not coming when called, has become ingrained. Don't get discouraged; just remember to practice, practice, practice.

Should You Use Food?

Should you use food in training? Let's face it, a great many dogs are far more effectively motivated to work for treats than they are for a pat on the head. I invite owners to observe their dogs' reactions when food is involved. When you pick up the dog treat box and your pet hears the treats shaking around inside, does she come streaking to you? When you show your dog a treat or your dog thinks you have one, is she focused like a laser beam? Will your dog ignore most everything else going on around her if she thinks treats are forthcoming from you? If the answer to any of these questions is yes, then food will likely work very well with your dog. If the answer is no (and some dogs are not food motivated), you need to find something that does motivate your dog.

Some dogs are ball crazy. They would rather fetch a ball or play with a toy like a Kong or a Rhino than get a treat. If this is your dog, give her five or ten seconds of quick play as a reward.

Some dogs aren't motivated by toys or food. They would rather just get petted. If this is your dog, then the big reward will be a nice five- to ten-second pet and/or scratch. The key isn't food, it's finding the strongest conditioned reinforcer. Do you remember what that is? If not, go back to Chapter 3.

If you use treats, you need to understand and master a few rules. You should use something small—half the size of your thumbnail for dogs 35 to 55 pounds, slightly larger for bigger breeds and smaller for dogs under 35 pounds. The reason for this is twofold. First, we're

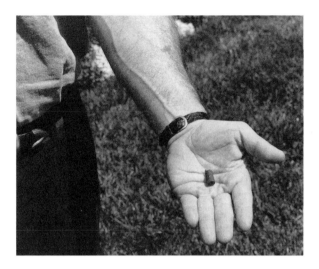

This is the right size food treat.

going to be doing a lot of repetitions and you don't want your dog to gain weight as a result of training, nor do you want to spoil her appetite for her nutritious main meals. Second, small treats are less distracting. The objective is to avoid making the focus of a training exercise the treats. The perfect food treat gives the dog a quick, tantalizing taste of something yummy. It is not something the dog needs 30 seconds to eat.

Treats should also be relatively odorless. It is also important to keep food treats hidden until the instant you give them to your dog. If you keep small, odorless treats hidden, your dog will not visually focus on the treats. This is an important point, and one many owners misunderstand. All too often, owners hold a big treat in plain view and encourage their dog to come get it. I can just picture you shaking a huge box of dog biscuits. The problem is, when you don't have the big treat in plain view, many dogs are far less inclined to respond.

For years, many trainers believed that using food in obedience training was a bad idea. Part of the reason for this was a belief that the dog would become dependent on the food and not work without it. This will not happen if the food is used correctly. By "correctly," I mean you must keep it hidden. By the way, for those of you using toys, you'll need to keep those hidden as well.

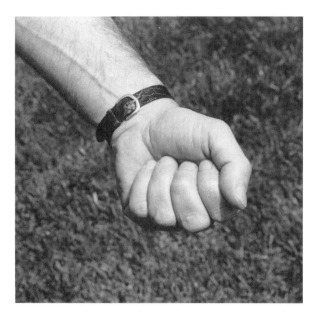

*Notice how easily a small food treat
can be concealed in your hand.*

Another reason trainers had problems using food relates to the schedule they recommended their students use in weaning the dogs off the food rewards. Frequently, trainers would go from having owners use food 100 percent of the time to zero—in the same session! This was much too rapid, and inevitably resulted in a poorer response when the food wasn't used. A bit later we will discuss how to properly wean dogs off food rewards, so that they work as well without them as they do with them.

First Assignment: Days 1 Through 7

Seven to 10 "come game" sessions per day, with five to 15 repetitions per session.

Getting back to teaching "come." The first step to teaching an off-leash "come" is to play what I call the "come game." Squat down, and in a happy, excited way quickly say "puppy, puppy, puppy" or your dog's name three or four times. You can clap your hands, or gently pat them on the ground, or on your legs. If your dog is sensitive to noise or a bit timid, try to keep your voice low and less excited.

Most dogs will come to you if you call them in this way. As your dog comes toward you, continue to coax her and show your excitement by speaking in a happy, positive tone. When your dog reaches you, pet her, praise her (say "good") and give the dog a small treat.

Please note that at no time during this sequence is the command "come" given.

What I've described here is one single repetition of the "come game." Try to do five to 15 repetitions in a short, positive training session. Don't make it too long or the dog will lose interest. Try to do seven to 10 training sessions per day. This sounds like a lot, but it's really not. Remember, a single session will probably take one to three minutes, so you might spend 30 minutes a day working on this all-important command. For most of you, that's no more time than you'll spend chasing after an untrained dog.

On the eighth day, we will advance further. By now, when you squat down and start to coax your dog, she should be highly motivated to come to you. During this next week, two variations of the come game will be added.

Second Assignment: Days 8 Through 14

Backing up game, five to 10 repetitions per session, for five to 10 sessions per day. Group come, 15 to 20 repetitions, two to five sessions per day.

Variation One: The Backing Up Come Game

The backing up come game is an excellent beginning "come" exercise. The purpose of this exercise is to increase the amount of time the dog focuses on you while coming to you.

Start off using the standard come game, but when the dog gets roughly three feet from you, stand up and back away approximately three to ten feet. As you're backing up, continue to coax the dog toward you and praise as the dog follows you. If the dog stops moving toward you, stop backing up, squat down again and resume coaxing.

Don't back up more than 10 feet or the dog may lose interest. You don't have to back up in a straight line, and in fact, it's a good idea to back up in zigzag patterns. When the dog reaches you, pet, praise (say "good") and if you're using food, give the dog a treat. If you're not using food, use whatever conditioned reinforcer works best for your dog. If you're using food, keep it hidden and use it 100 percent of the time. Do this exercise five to 10 times per session, five to 10 sessions per day.

It is also important that your dog learns to be comfortable when you reach out and grasp her collar when she gets to you. Make this easy and nonthreatening. Don't lunge at the dog and grab the collar. Instead, gently grasp it as you're petting, praising and treating. This is important, because it is inevitable that at some point in your dog's life you will need to grab hold of her collar. Usually it's to stop her from running or walking into a dangerous situation. If you condition your dog to associate positive things with you grabbing her collar, you will be far less likely to wind up with a dog who bolts when you reach for her. Remember to add this to the end of each come game repetition.

Crouch down to start the backing up "come" game.

Here is the beginning of the "come" game sequence with the dog.

*Stand up and back up as the dog comes
toward you. See how responsive this dog is.*

*Get the dog used to having her
collar grasped when she comes.*

And don't forget to praise, praise, praise.

Variation Two: Group Come Game

Some owners find that after the first couple of come game repetitions, the dog starts following them around. This makes it very difficult to move far enough away to coax your dog to you in the first place. If this happens, enlist the help of a friend or family member and play a group come game.

The group come game is simple enough. One person stands approximately 10 to 15 feet away from the other. The first person (it doesn't matter who) coaxes the dog. When the dog reaches them, they should pet, praise (say "good") and treat. At that point, the second person squats and coaxes, which will likely stimulate the dog to come to them. If the dog doesn't respond because she is still focused on the first person, that person should stand up, stop praising and petting, and ignore the dog. The second person should continue to coax, at which point the dog will go to them. When the dog reaches the second person, they should pet, praise (say "good") and treat.

Two people can encourage the dog to go back and forth between them dozens of times. Some dogs pick up on this exercise very quickly and, without coaxing, start running back and forth between the people. There is nothing wrong with this. Each person should remember to squat, pet, praise (say "good") and treat. The objective here is to reward the behavior of the dog coming to you.

Don't do this exercise for too long at one time, or the dog will become bored. It's always best to end a training session with your

The group come game with two people.

dog wanting more. After 15 to 20 repetitions, stop the exercise (one repetition is when the dog goes to each person once). Try doing five sessions per day, and remember to do the backing up come game as well.

Third Assignment: Days 15 Through 20

Backing up game with "come" command when the dog is one foot away; five to 10 repetitions per session, five to 10 sessions per day. Group come with "come" command when the dog is one foot away; 15 to 20 repetitions per session, two to five sessions per day. Remember to stop squatting starting on day 17.

Variation Three: Standing Up and Adding Commands

By the beginning of the third week, you can start to add the verbal command "come" in situations where it is impossible for the dog to fail. The best way to ensure this is to wait until the dog is no more than a foot away from you before you actually give the "come" command. This is a critical point. If you command too soon and the dog stops or doesn't come all the way, you really have no way to avoid teaching the dog that there's no need to come to you without delay. You are much better off commanding when the dog is almost all the way to you. The purpose of this is to teach the dog to associate a very positive act (coming to you) with the command. The stronger this association, the better off you will be.

For the next week, your two exercises (back up come game and group come) will remain the same, except:

1. Add the "come" command at the end of each repetition.

2. Starting on day 17, you can stop squatting and simply bend slightly as you coax your dog to you. If the dog doesn't respond to coaxing when you're not squatting, resume squatting for another week before you try this again.

Remember, continue to lightly grasp the collar after the "come" command is given. Food is still rewarded 100 percent of the time and remains hidden.

When the dog has mastered coming to you when you're standing up, you can add a "sit" command.

Fourth Assignment: Days 21 Through 27

Backing up game with "come" command when your dog is two feet away; five to 10 repetitions per session, five to 10 sessions per day. Group come game with distractions; seven to 15 repetitions per session, three to five sessions per day.

By now you have had three solid weeks of teaching your dog some critical lessons. These include:

◆ A positive association with coming to you

◆ Connecting the command "come" to the act of coming to you (at least for the last week)

◆ A positive association with having her collar grasped

Hopefully, there has been little or no inconsistency in the way the command "come" was given. If you've done this properly, then at this point when you coax your dog, chances are she comes zipping to you in a very positive way. And why not? You've done this hundreds and hundreds of times. Now it's time to add distractions.

Variation Four: Adding Distractions

Have a friend or family member stand off to the side with something that will likely distract the dog. It could be a large bone or a sandwich. It could also be a ball or a favorite toy. Squeaky toys are often excellent for this type of exercise. You can also get creative. It might be an adult holding a child or a cat or another dog. Please note that if you are using toys to motivate or reward your dog for coming, then the distracter can't use toys to distract your dog.

While your distracter (the person creating the distractions) stands to one side, you gently hold the dog's collar and pet and praise her. A third person stands 15 to 20 feet away, so that the distracter is roughly halfway between you and the third person.

Let go of the dog and have the third person squat and coax the dog to come. If you've done your homework consistently, about 90 percent of the time your dog will ignore the distracter and head right for the third person. Needless to say, the third person needs to coax, pet, praise (say "good") and reward the dog for coming. The verbal command can still be given when the dog is one foot away, with you grasping the collar during praise, petting and treating. After a few days, if you're getting a consistent response, stop squatting and just coax from a slightly bent standing position.

The distracter should try to distract the dog, but not in a way that causes confusion. For example, distracters must not squat and/or coax the dog. Additionally, they must be careful not to do anything that would reward the dog for not coming to you or the third person—for instance, if the distracter has food and this food is held low to the ground, the dog might get it. If this happens, you will likely set your training back, since your dog will be rewarded by getting food as a result of straying over to the distracter.

Even though the distracter can't confuse the dog, there's a lot the distracter can do. Keys can be dropped, squeaky toys squeaked, food visually presented, etc. If the dog goes to the distracter, the person coaxing should continue to coax and the distracter should immediately stop any distracting behavior. In the case of food or a toy, the distracter should hold it well out of the dog's reach and out of sight, ideally over her head. This will ensure that your dog will not be rewarded for being distracted.

It's a good idea to start with the distracter using easy types of distractions, and gradually build up to more difficult ones. For example, if the dog is food motivated, you might start with the distracter holding a toy or squeezing a squeaky toy, then move up to holding a piece of food close to their chest, and then to waving a big bone.

When you first try this exercise, some dogs will spend 20 or 30 seconds sniffing around the distracter. Don't worry. Just keep coaxing her, and remember to reward and praise the dog when she comes. Try seven to 15 repetitions per session, with three to five sessions per day. Remember on this exercise to use food rewards 100 percent of the time. Eventually the dog will ignore anything the distracter does.

Continue to play the backing up come game, as well. However, starting this week, instead of giving the "come" command when the dog is one foot from you, give it when the dog is two feet away.

The Second Month

Moving into the second month, a number of improvements will be added to the "come" concept. First, you will start to use the command when the dog is farther and farther away from you. Second, you will start to wean the dog off food rewards.

At this point, you are working on some exercises with no distractions and others with distractions. Assuming you've done this consistently, most owners should have close to 100 percent response with no distractions. This means when you coax your dog, she comes zipping to you every time. If your dog falls into this category, you're going to start to do what the top trainer at Animal Behavior College, Debbie Kendrick, calls "upping the ante." This means you are going to stop rewarding the dog 100 percent of the time with food or play. Instead, you are going to reward only the best responses. This will cause the dog to work that much harder to receive the reward. You will slowly continue to up the ante, meaning you will only reward better and better responses.

Variation Five: Teaching Come From a Distance, Weaning Off Food, Continuing to Work With Distractions

To start off, do the group come game with distractions. Watch your dog. When she comes to you, does she sometimes come quickly and other times stop to sniff or come more slowly to you? If yes, she should only receive the food reward for coming quickly. *This does not mean she shouldn't be praised and petted for coming.* It simply means the food or toy reward should be withheld until you see the more desired fast response.

If speed isn't an issue, look at other possible weaknesses. Does the dog sniff and stop during some part of the come game? If so, when the dog does get to you, praise and pet, but don't treat. Only treat when the dog goes directly to you without sniffing. Does the dog veer off and go to the distracter? If yes, only treat those responses in which the dog comes straight to you without veering.

It's best to pick one "mistake" at a time to not treat. Otherwise, you may find yourself not being able to treat at all. This is not desirable. I recommend grading the dog's response. Let's look at an example.

- ◆ **Grade A:** The dog comes within one second of hearing her name. She comes straight to you without pausing, sniffing or veering off, regardless of distractions. She moves quickly and comes all the way to you, allowing you to grasp her collar. She does this from distances up to 40 feet away.

- ◆ **Grade B:** The dog comes within one second of hearing her name. She comes straight to you, although she may slow down sometimes to sniff or look at a distraction. She does not veer and comes all the way to you, allowing you to grasp her collar. She does this from distances up to 30 feet away.

- ◆ **Grade C:** The dog comes within one to two seconds of hearing her name. She comes to you, although at times she may slow down to sniff and/or veer off to check out a particularly interesting distraction. She eventually comes all the way to you, allowing you to grasp her collar. Occasionally she may run past you or only come within two or three feet before starting to run back in the other direction. She performs from distances up to 25 feet away.

◆ **Grade D:** The dog comes within one to five seconds of hearing her name. She comes to you, although at times she may slow down to sniff and/or veer off to check out a particularly interesting distraction. Sometimes, she will pause for as much as 15 or 20 seconds around a distraction. You continue to coax and she eventually comes all the way to you, allowing you to grasp her collar. Occasionally she may run past you or only come within two or three feet before starting to run back in the other direction. She performs from distances up to 20 feet away.

If your dog is not performing at least at grade D with a distracter, you need to continue to work on the earlier exercises to make sure you have established the foundation level of understanding before you move on. If your dog is performing at least at grade D, you can use food to improve the dog's performance, while at the same time slowly weaning the dog off the treats.

Please remember, toys as motivators should be handled the same way as treats. And if your dog is best motivated by simple petting, you should not withhold petting but rather cut down on the duration and excitement you show when petting your dog. This means a grade D response might get a pat on the head and a quick "good dog," while a grade C response would get a scratch behind the ear for 10 seconds as you repeat "good dog" in a more excited way the entire time you're scratching.

To move from grade D to grade C, simply treat only grade C responses or better. Since most grade D dogs will perform the "come" at grade C some of the time, treating grade C responses will result in the dog very quickly understanding what she needs to do to get the treat. This is an extremely important concept.

Once the dog advances to a point where she is consistently (90 percent of the time) working at a grade C level, start to treat only when the dog works at a grade B level. The same rules apply.

Once the dog is working consistently at grade B, stay there for an extra week and start using the "come" command when the dog is four feet away, instead of two. This has no bearing on when you give a treat; it's simply a good time to start increasing the distance your dog is from you when she actually hears the command. Increase by one foot per week, until you are giving the command at the 30- to 40-foot mark.

After the dog is consistently responding for an extra week at grade B, advance to grade A using the same treat schedule. Try different distractions, and if the dog's grade slips, work it back up. When you have a grade A response from distances of 40 feet, regardless of distractions, in house and yard, you have foundation level control off leash on the "come" command.

You can also continue to reward better and better responses with food, until the dog is at a level you're satisfied with. At that point, slowly wean the dog from the treats by reducing them 10 percent each week, until you reach the 20 percent mark. This means the dog gets food at grade A level only 20 percent of the time.

I deliberately devoted the most space and detail to the "come" command because I believe it to be the most important, and because the concepts of giving rewards and consistency remain the same for the other commands as well. Although "come" is most important, other commands are critical for your dog to learn.

SIT

The first rule in teaching an off-leash sit is to become aware of how many times you tell your dog to sit without follow-through. Just like the "come" command, owners need to become conscious of just how often they tell their dogs to "sit, sit, sit." Many of you may be surprised when you realize you're telling your dog to do just that, dozens of times each day. After a few days of really becoming aware of it, the first order of business is for everyone to stop giving the "sit" command under any circumstances other than the ones described in this chapter.

Before teaching sit, or any obedience command, you will need to teach your dog the meaning of a conditioned reinforcer such as the word "good." If you are unclear about how to do this (hint, it's easy), please go back and read the section in Chapter 3 that covers conditioned reinforcers and how to teach them. Briefly, your dog wasn't born knowing what "good" means. She needs to be conditioned—that is, trained—to understand that "good" is positive for her. This is simple to do.

Once the dog has learned "good," you can start teaching her to sit. The best way to do this is to lure the dog with your baited hand. This means you put a small piece of food in your hand and make a fist. Hold your fist directly in front of the dog's nose. Let her sniff it, and then slowly bring your hand over the top of the dog's muzzle and head, and moving on down the center of the dog's back. Keep your hand no more than three to four inches from the dog, especially when it's by her muzzle and head. Most dogs will lift their head in an attempt to follow your hand. As your hand moves out of sight they will continue to look backward, and as they shift their body in the direction your hand is moving, they will sit.

First, I get Buford's attention.

*Then I bring my hand over the top of his head
and move it slowly backward, toward his tail.*

The results are plain to see. Buford is sitting—just like a real dog.

The moment the dog is in the sit position, pet, praise (say "good") and treat. If treats are not actually a huge motivator, you can show the dog a toy, hide it in your fist, bring your hand back as I've just described, and when the dog sits, pet, praise (say "good") and reward with five to 10 seconds of play with the previously hidden toy. Do not say "sit" at any time during this exercise. Try 20 to 30 repetitions per day, with no more than five repetitions at any one time. After one or two weeks, your dog should be sitting the instant you start to bring your hand over the top of her head.

When you consistently get this level of response, add the command. To do this, wait until the dog has actually sat, and the instant she does, say "sit," pet, praise (say "good") and treat. Do this for another two weeks at the rate of 20 to 30 repetitions per day.

By the second month, you can start to say "sit" a second before you bring your hand over the top of the dog's head. Don't say "sit" and then fail to use your hand. If you've done your homework, the dog will sit every single time, since you've already gotten 100 percent (or close) compliance using just your hand. Do this for another two weeks, and then you can start adding distractions.

When you add distractions, go back a step and only say "sit" after the dog has sat. Basically, use a distracter the same way I described earlier in this chapter for teaching "come." The only difference is the distracter doesn't need to be 10 or 15 feet away. They can be closer, but otherwise should act in the same way as described for "come." If the dog fails to respond, don't worry. Simply get the dog to refocus on your hand and repeat the exercise. The distracter should stop the instant you see that they have been successful in distracting the dog. This will enable you to get a better response.

Start off with easy distractions and build up. After a couple of weeks, your dog should sit regardless of what the distracter is doing. At this point, you can start to grade "sit" the same way you graded "come."

◆ **Grade A:** The dog sits within one second of the command without using your hands, regardless of distractions in the house and yard.

- ◆ **Grade B:** The dog sits within one to three seconds of the command without using your hands, regardless of distractions in the house and yard.

- ◆ **Grade C:** The dog sits within one second of the command as you bring your hand over the top of the dog's head, regardless of distractions in the house and yard.

- ◆ **Grade D:** The dog sits within one to three seconds of the command as you bring your hand over the top of the dog's head. When the delay occurs, it is because the dog briefly focuses on the distraction.

If your dog is not performing at least at grade D level, you need to continue to work on the sit using food 100 percent of the time, until you get at least a D level response.

To move from grade D to grade C, simply treat the dog only for grade C responses. Since most grade D dogs will perform the sit at grade C at least some of the time, treating grade C responses will result in the dog very quickly understanding what she needs to do to receive the treat. This is an extremely important concept.

Once the dog advances to a point where she is consistently (90 percent of the time) working at a grade C level, start to treat only when the dog works at a grade B level.

To move up to grade B, a professional tip is in order. At grade C the dog is responding to your hand gesture. At grade B no hand gesture is given. This can be a big jump for some dogs. Additionally, you have to deliberately avoid making the gesture, so the dog can learn to respond without it, which is something you haven't yet done. To move to grade B, give the "sit" command and wait one long second without making any gesture at all. If you've done your homework, your dog will likely sit in anticipation of the gesture. The instant the dog sits, pet, praise (say "good") and reward. If the dog fails to sit after one second, start the gesture, but then stop the instant the dog sits. You will probably only need to move your hand a couple of inches to get a response. Note how much you need to move your hand and gradually move it less, only treating when the dog sits at the smallest gestures. Eventually you won't need to use your hand at all.

Once the dog is working consistently at grade B, advance to grade A using the same treat schedule. Try different distractions, and if the dog's grade slips, work it back up. When you have a grade A response while you're standing in front of the dog, you can start to move away from the dog. If you've done this properly, most dogs will respond even if you give the command when you're standing off to one side. It is best to start teaching sit from different positions by working with no distractions, until the dog responds perfectly for a few days. Then add distractions while you give the "sit" command from these positions.

When the dog sits perfectly under all types of distractions, regardless of your position, try making it a little tougher. You can call this grade A+. Give the sit command when you're standing behind the dog. Many dogs will find this tougher, since all your previous work was done with you in sight. You can also continue to reward better and better responses with food, until the dog is at a level you're satisfied with. At that point, slowly wean the dog from the treats by reducing them 10 percent per week, until you reach the 20 percent mark. This means the dog gets food for a grade A level performance only 20 percent of the time.

If your dog doesn't respond at any point, try two or three more repetitions to get the response. Reward the proper response. If, after two to three repetitions, she remains unresponsive, end the session and try again later. When you stop, avoid any interaction with the dog for at least 15 minutes. This is not to punish the dog, but you also don't want to reward her for not working. The best thing to do is simply walk away and do something unrelated to her.

SIT-STAY

The sit-stay command is also a very critical behavior for your dog to learn. Like all the other off-leash commands you're teaching, it's important to recognize that you may already be giving the sit-stay command without backing it up. Spend a few days being conscious of this and you may be very surprised to realize there has been some inconsistency here. Not to worry! The key is to move forward from this point.

By the way, here's an excellent example of inconsistency with the sit-stay. I have known at least a hundred owners whose dogs wanted to follow them into the garage or out the front door when the owners were leaving for work. A typical response for people is to shove the dog back and tell her "no, stay." Then they close the door and go on with their day. Hours later when they come home, do they seriously expect their dog to still be in the stay position? Of course not! They didn't mean "stay" as in "don't move." They meant something like "don't follow me out the door." Unfortunately, this sets back your training, since the dog will not be able to differentiate these subtle shades of gray. Bottom line: "Stay" means "don't move until I tell you to." Don't use it for anything else.

I would not teach "stay" until the dog has had at least a month's worth of training on "sit." The two easiest situations to start teaching the sit-stay are when you are feeding the dog and when she wants to go through a doorway.

When you are ready to give her a meal, hold the bowl up three or four feet over her head and tell her "sit." Remember to praise (say "good") for the sit, but you don't have to treat and pet with a food bowl in your hand. As she's sitting, slowly start to bring the bowl down toward her and the floor. If she gets up, say "no" or "eh eh" and immediately raise the bowl back over her head. Do not let her get the food. Then have her sit again and repeat the process. You may need to repeat this five to 10 times before you can successfully bring the bowl down to the floor without her getting up from the sit position and moving toward the bowl.

Be ready to block the bowl if she dives for it and put it far enough away that you have a real chance of successfully keeping it away from her. The objective here is not to tease the dog. However, if she is rewarded for grabbing the food when you really want to teach her to stay, you won't succeed. After one second of her staying in the sit position with the bowl on the ground, tell her "OK" and stand aside so she can get her meal. Most dogs will instantly get the idea of "OK" as a word that releases them from a command.

*I tell the dog "sit" and start to
place the bowl on the floor.*

*If the dog stands up from the sit
or moves toward me from a
stand position, I immediately
raise the bowl out of reach.*

*Eventually, I am able to put the bowl
on the floor while the dog stays.*

*This dog really gets it. He isn't
focused on the food bowl at all.*

Do not give the "stay" command until your dog can successfully perform this exercise for seven consecutive days. This means your dog remains seated when you place the bowl on the ground. It also means she waits a long second before you release her with "OK." After seven consecutive successful days, you can say "stay" before you start to bring the food bowl down, since you now know the dog will not move.

The door exercise is very similar to the food bowl exercise. Approach a door you know the dog wants to go through. (Please don't start teaching this concept at a front door leading to a busy street. Use a door that you can afford to make a few mistakes with and not put the dog's safety in jeopardy.) Start to open the door, then quickly shut it the instant the dog starts to put her nose through it. Be careful! The objective here is not to slam the door on the dog's nose. Carefully open and shut the door until the dog sits down away from it. If the dog just stands back away from the door without sitting, you may give the "sit" command. Remember to pet, praise (say "good") and treat for this response.

After a week or two of this, your dog should sit when you open the door. If the dog gets up as you open the door, say "no" or "eh eh," quickly close the door and have the dog sit again. Once the dog is sitting and has been petted, praised and rewarded for this behavior, open the door again. Most dogs will grasp the idea that they need to remain seated. After one long second, close the door and release the dog with an "OK." If the dog continues to sit there, you can playfully push the dog out of the sit.

Please note you don't need to do this near every door in the house. I would practice it with a few doors 10 to 15 times per day. Remember, don't say "stay" until the dog is consistently performing this exercise (90 percent of the time) for at least a week. You can then add the "stay" command during the one second the dog should stay.

After the second week, you can start to slowly increase the amount of time the dog stays. To do this, wait five seconds instead of one before releasing the dog with "OK." Does the dog do this with no problem? If yes, add another five seconds the next day. If no, keep working on it.

At first, open the door slightly.

If the dog tries to escape,
quickly close the door.

After a couple of weeks, you can make the door exercise a little bit more difficult. Have the dog sit, then place yourself between the dog and the door. Since most people stand next to their dog when they're first working on the door exercise, moving in front of the dog may initially cause the dog to stand up. If she does, tell her "no" or "eh eh," have her sit, pet, praise and reward the sit response, then repeat the process. Face the dog, carefully open the door and start to back through it. If the dog moves at this time, say "no" or "eh eh," block her with your legs, close the door, have her sit and repeat the process. Start with a one-second stay. After a week, you can start to add time.

Only give the "stay" command when the dog is consistently performing this exercise properly for at least a week. Only release her with an "OK" to go through the door when she is sitting and not trying to bolt. After a month of working on these exercises, your dog should have an off-leash understanding of the "stay" concept. If you have doubts, work the above exercises for another week, or as long as it takes for the dog to perform them properly.

During the second month, you can add a third sit-stay exercise. This involves a food treat. Have the dog sit. Remember to pet, praise (say "good") and treat. Then place another treat in your hand and show it to the dog by holding it two or three feet from her face. If she moves toward it, say "no" or "eh eh" and quickly close your hand. Have her sit again, remembering to pet, praise and treat, then start over. Most dogs will stop moving toward the treat after a few repetitions. When you can present the treat and she doesn't move toward it for at least one long second, say "good" and bring the treat to her. Pet her and let her eat the snack. Then release her with an "OK." Try to work this exercise at least 15 or 20 times a day for at least a week.

Remember, don't say "stay" for the first week. Then, assuming your dog is performing this exercise without mistakes at least 90 percent of the time, you can say "stay" while the dog is sitting and watching the food. If you do it correctly, your dog will remain seated for a long second with food two feet from her face. By the third week, you can start to increase the amount of time the dog stays. Jump to five seconds and add five seconds every day until you reach a couple of minutes. Make it pleasant and make sure the dog is consistently rewarded with food treats for the correct response.

Teaching your dog to stay in this fashion is, in my opinion, much better than the way it used to be taught. What we are doing is training the dog to stay in order to get something. This could include a food treat, dinner or going through a door. This is the opposite of teaching her to stay to avoid being punished. It's much more positive and will elicit a far more willing response from the dog.

After a few months of simple sit-stays at doors, for dinner and when food is presented in front of her face, you should have a dog who understands the concept of "stay." As you continue to add more time to your dog's stay, you can also start to use a grading system and add distractions.

- ◆ **Grade A:** The dog stays for at least two minutes, regardless of distractions, in the house or yard.

- ◆ **Grade B:** The dog stays for at least a minute with all but the most difficult distractions.

- ◆ **Grade C:** The dog stays for a minute and a half without distractions (other than the food bowl, doors or food in front of her face).

- ◆ **Grade D:** The dog stays for a minute without distractions (other than the food bowl, doors or food in front of her face).

If your dog is not performing at least at grade D level, you need to continue to work on the sit-stay using food rewards 100 percent of the time, until you get at least a D level response.

To move from grade D to grade C, simply treat only grade C responses. Since most grade D dogs can perform the stay at grade C at least some of the time, increase the time by 30-second increments and treat only grade C responses. The dog will very quickly understand what she needs to do to receive the treat. This is an extremely important concept.

Once the dog advances to a point where she is consistently (90 percent of the time) working at a grade C level, start to only treat when the dog works at a grade B level. To move to grade B, start off with relatively easy distractions and expect a stay for maybe 20 seconds with these types of distractions. If you can get this, pet, praise, but don't treat. Then try 40 seconds, rewarding the dog the same way. Give the dog a break, then about five minutes later, try again and aim for a minute. When the dog stays for a minute with mild distractions, pet, praise and treat. If you've done your homework, your dog will respond at this level.

Once the dog is working consistently at grade B, advance to grade A using the same treat schedule. Try different distractions, and if the dog's grade slips, work it back up.

Your position in relation to the dog is as relevant for "stay" as it was for "sit." As such, the same rules apply. When you have a grade A response standing in front of the dog, you can start to move away from the dog. If you've done this correctly, most dogs will respond even if you give the stay command when standing off to one side. It is best to start teaching stay from different positions by working on it with no distractions until the dog responds perfectly for a few days. Then add distractions while you give the stay command from these positions as well. When the dog stays perfectly under all types of distractions regardless of your position, try making it a little tougher. You can call this grade A+. Give the stay command when you're standing behind the dog. Many dogs will find this more difficult since all your previous stay work was done with you in sight. You can also continue to reward better and better responses with food until the dog is at a level you're satisfied with. At that point, slowly wean the dog from the treats by reducing them 10 percent per week until you reach the 20 percent mark. This means the dog gets food for grade A level compliance only 20 percent of the time.

If your dog doesn't respond at any point, try two or three more repetitions to get the response. Reward the proper response. If, after two to three repetitions, she remains unresponsive, end the session and try again later. When you stop, avoid any interaction with the dog for at least 15 minutes. This is not to punish the dog, but you also don't want to reward her for not working. The best thing to do is simply walk away and do something unrelated to her.

When your dog attains foundation level obedience for the "stay," you will still need to work on this command with a leash and possibly a long line in a group class environment. However, since the foundation has been firmly established, you will most likely find "stay" is a very easy concept for your dog to grasp under any circumstances. "Stay" can be a lifesaver and is certainly one of the most important commands you can teach your dog.

DOWN

The final command we will focus on for off-leash foundation level control is "down." I probably sound like a broken record at this point—oh no, I'm giving my age away, but I know I'm repeating myself. Guess what? The "down" command has the same rules about consistency as all the others.

So what's the first step? If you guessed "you need to be conscious of how often you say 'down' without backing it up," you're absolutely right! A common example of inconsistency in using this command is when the owner tries to teach the dog to stay off furniture or not to jump on people. How many of you tell your dog "no, no, down, down, down" when the dog leaps all over you? Do you say the same thing when your adorable dog is lying on that leather chair you absolutely don't want her on? All use of the command "down" should stop now, except as recommended in this chapter.

"Down" should not be taught until the dog has mastered the "sit" command. This means the dog sits at least at grade B.

The traditional way to teach "down" involved forcing the dog into that position. Methods involving stepping on the leash and/or sharply yanking the leash downward were common. Forcing some dogs, especially dogs older than a year, into the down position can stimulate aggression, distrust and an unwillingness to obey the "down" command, especially when you don't have the leash. Fortunately, you can teach this concept with little or no force off the leash. This is a much better way.

The challenge with "down" is that it represents a vulnerable and subservient position for a dog. Men should consider how they would feel being shaved by a total stranger. Yes, you know the barber is a professional, but when that straight-edged razor is lightly scraping across your neck, you can't help feeling vulnerable. To be honest, when I wrote this book, I tried for 20 minutes to think of a similar example for a woman. While I have no doubt my women readers will come up with a number of them instantly, I drew a blank. However, I think and hope all readers get the idea. "Down" makes some dogs just a wee bit uncomfortable. Because of this, it can sometimes be challenging to get them into the down position without resorting to force.

Here are several ways:

1. From the "sit" position, lure the dog down with a baited hand. Stand directly in front of the dog. Just as with "sit," put a piece of food in your fist and hold your fist in front of the dog's nose. Then slowly bring your hand down close to her chest until your hand touches the ground. At that point, slowly move your hand along the ground toward you. Most dogs will follow your hand with their nose. When their nose touches or comes close to the ground, they will continue to follow your hand as you move it away from them and toward yourself. This will cause the dog to lean

I am standing to the side, but my hand is
still directly in front of the dog's face.

forward. At that point, most dogs will lie down. The instant the dog lies down, pet, praise (say "good") and treat.

This method can be a little trickier than it sounds, and you should be aware of a few common mistakes. First, move your hand *slowly*. If you go too quickly, the dog won't follow it. Second, bring your hand straight down and touch the ground before you start to move it toward you. Often owners bring their hand toward themselves before it touches the ground. This will cause the dog to stand up and follow your hand. Third, don't stand too far away from the dog when you try this. I would stand no more than a foot or two away, directly in front of the dog.

2. Even if you use your hand perfectly, some dogs are inclined to get up if you're standing directly in front of them. If you find your dog repeatedly standing up and moving toward you, consider positioning yourself immediately at the dog's side. The exercise is done the same way, except when your hand touches the ground, you're not moving it toward yourself. Instead, you simply move it slowly in a straight line away from the dog. Remember to pet, praise (say "good") and treat the instant the dog lies down.

As I bring my hand to the gound, the dog
follows my hand into the "down" position.

*I never forget to praise and
treat an excellent response.*

3. Another way to teach "down" from the sit position is to use a food lure to guide the dog under a very low object, such as a coffee table or, for smaller dogs, your outstretched leg while you're sitting on the floor. Some dogs like to stand up even when you do the exercise correctly, and using the coffee table or your leg prevents this. Remember to pet, praise (say "good") and treat the instant the dog lies down.

Again, regardless of which variation you try, the moment the dog's elbows touch the ground, pet, praise (say "good") and place the food treat on the ground between her paws. Once you've determined which variation works best for you and your dog, use that variation 15 to 20 times per day for approximately two weeks. Remember not to say "down" at any time during this exercise. And please remember to not teach down every time you give the sit command. If you do, your dog will start to lie down after you've told her to sit.

Professional tip: Be mindful of the surface on which you attempt to teach the down. Pavement is hard, and it's hot in the summer, cold in the winter. Uncomfortable surfaces make this command more difficult to teach. I recommend grass or carpeting to start. It's soft and comfortable, and who wouldn't want to lie down on it?

Don't give the "down" command until your dog consistently goes into the down position when you move your hand to the ground for at least two weeks. At that point, you can say "down" the instant the dog's elbows touch the ground, and immediately follow the command with petting, praise ("good") and a treat. Stay at this level for another two weeks.

After a month of teaching the down command, you should be ready to expand how you use it. This includes teaching the dog to respond to the command without the hand gesture, teaching her to work with distractions and keeping the dog in the down position (down-stay).

By the second month, you can start to say "down" a second before you bring your hand to the ground. Don't say "down" without using your hand. If you've done your homework, the dog will lie down just about every single time, since you've already gotten 100 percent compliance (or close) with just your hand. After a week of practicing using both the command and the hand signal, try giving the "down" command and not moving your hand. If your dog consistently lies down, congratulations! This command can be tough to teach.

If the dog still seems a bit confused when you don't use your hand, don't be discouraged. Instead, work on giving the down command and waiting one long second before using your hand signal. Also notice about how far your hand motion has to go before the dog lies down. Are you bringing your hand all the way to the ground? Are you still moving it away from the dog? Many people find that all they have to do is move their hand a couple of inches toward the ground to get the desired response. If your dog still needs a hand signal of any kind, use it after the command has been given for another two or three weeks before trying the "down" command again without the gesture. Do this for another two weeks, and then you can start to add distractions.

When you add distractions, go back a step and only say "down" after the dog has attained that position. In other words, resume having the dog lie down by using your hand gesture. Basically, use a designated distracter the same way I described in the section on teaching "come." The only difference is this person need not be 10 or 15 feet away. They can be closer, but otherwise should act in the same way as I described for "come."

If the dog fails to respond in the presence of distractions, don't worry. Get the dog to refocus on your hand and simply repeat the exercise. The distracter should stop the instant you see that they have been successful in distracting the dog. This will enable you to get a better response.

Start off with easy distractions and build up. After a couple of weeks, your dog should lie down regardless of what the distracter is doing. At this point, reintroduce the verbal command *before* the hand gesture. You can also start to grade the "down" the way you graded other commands.

- ◆ **Grade A:** The dog lies down within one second of your command without using your hands, regardless of distractions in the house and yard.

- ◆ **Grade B:** The dog lies down within one to three seconds of your command without using your hands, regardless of distractions in the house and yard.

- ◆ **Grade C:** The dog lies down within one second of your command as you bring your hand toward the ground, regardless of distractions in the house and yard.

- ◆ **Grade D:** The dog lies down within one to three seconds of your command as you bring your hand toward the ground. Sometimes she fails to respond to the first gesture when there are distractions.

If your dog is not performing at least at grade D level, you need to continue to work on the down using food rewards 100 percent of the time until you get at least a D level response.

To move from grade D to grade C, simply treat only grade C responses. Since most grade D dogs will perform the down at grade C at least some of the time, treating grade C responses will result in the dog very quickly understanding what she needs to do to receive the treat.

Once the dog advances to a point where she is consistently (90 percent of the time) working at a grade C level, start to treat only when the dog works at a grade B level. The same professional tip that I gave you to assist in advancing from grade C to B on the sit command will also work for down.

At grade C the dog is responding to your hand gesture. At grade B no hand gesture is given. This can be a big jump for some dogs. Additionally, you have to deliberately avoid making the gesture so the dog can learn to respond without it, which is something you haven't done before. To move to grade B, give the down command and wait one long second without making any gesture at all. If you've done your homework, your dog will likely lie down in anticipation of the gesture. The instant the dog lies down, pet, praise (say "good") and treat. If the dog fails to lie down after one second, start to make the gesture, but then stop the instant the dog lies down. You will probably only need to move your hand a couple of inches to get a response. Note how much you need to move your hand and gradually move it less, only treating when the dog lies down at the smallest gesture. Eventually you won't need to use your hand at all.

Once the dog is working consistently at grade B, advance to grade A using the same treat schedule. Try different distractions, and if the dog's grade slips, work it back up. When you consistently have a grade A response while you're standing in front of or at the dog's side, you can start to move away from the dog. If you've done this properly, most dogs will respond even if you give the command while you're standing in a different place.

It is best to start teaching "down" from different positions by working on it with no distractions, until the dog responds perfectly for a few days. It's also a good idea to start out close to the dog as you begin shifting your position. For example, if you taught the dog "down" from directly in front of her, your first new position should be directly at her side. If you taught her down from the side, the second position might be directly in front. Once the dog responds consistently to positions close to you, it is easier to teach her to lie down when you are farther away.

Next, add distractions while you give the down command from these alternate positions. When the dog lies down perfectly in the presence of all types of distractions, regardless of your position, use the A+ grade for the down command. This means have her lie down from a position where the dog can't see you—perhaps from behind her. Many dogs will find this tougher, since all the previous work on this command was done with you in sight. You can also continue to reward better and better responses with food, until the dog is at a level you're satisfied with. At that point, slowly wean the dog from the treats by reducing them 10 percent per week until you reach the 20 percent mark. This means the dog gets food for responses at grade A level only 20 percent of the time.

If your dog doesn't respond at any point, try two or three more repetitions to get the response. Reward the proper response. If, after two to three repetitions, she remains unresponsive, end the session and try again later. When you stop, avoid any interaction with the dog for at least 15 minutes. This is not to punish the dog, but you also don't want to reward her for not working. The best thing to do is simply walk away and do something unrelated to her.

Down-Stay

You can attach a "stay" command to the "down" once the "stay" and "down" have both been mastered. To do this, be conscious of your timing and what you praise and reward the dog for doing.

Tell the dog to lie down, pet, praise (say "good") and treat. Then tell the dog to stay. Wait 10 seconds, then pet, praise (say "good") and treat. Wait another two seconds and give the dog the "OK" release command. If the dog breaks the stay before you release her, immediately say "no" or "eh eh," have the dog lie back down and then give proper praise and petting. Then repeat the process. Practice this for a couple of days, then start to add time until you get to a minute or so. Then add distractions.

When your dog lies down on the first command and stays there for as long as you'd like, regardless of distractions, you have an extremely functional command. Try teaching the dog to do a down-stay on a three- or four-foot piece of carpeting. I did this with one of my dogs many years ago. It was great, because the carpeting (her spot) was completely portable. I could take her spot anywhere I wanted, place it on the ground and know that if I asked, she'd go to her spot and lie there. I could take her to people's homes, to a variety of public places, and know that she was safe and out of trouble on her spot.

I actually used this "trick" in front of various supermarkets when I first started my business. I would take my dog, a beautiful white Samoyed named Samantha, and place her spot three or four feet from the front door. I would then have her lie on it while I posted training flyers. When I went to the other side of the market (some had two bulletin boards), I would bring her spot with me and put her there. People were very amused when they saw this, and many wanted to know how I had done it. When they realized I was a dog trainer, they wanted me to show them how to do it, which was great for business. (Of course, this trick isn't as good as my Basset Hound jumping through an extremely low hoop. Actually, he doesn't really jump, he just sort of ambles through it. However, that's a story for another time.)

As you can see by reading this chapter, teaching and getting foundation level control should start as early as possible and can take many months to master. I can assure all of you that it is absolutely worth doing, so start today! If you've done it all correctly, you should have a dog who sits, stays, comes and lies down off leash in your house and yard on the first command, regardless of distractions. If you honestly have that level of response, congratulations! You have built a foundation that will last as long as your dog lives.

At this point, you are about 40 percent through the training process. What's next? Finding a professional trainer to help you teach loose leash walking and/or heel, and to help you train your dog to respond to all the foundation level commands around distractions in public. Remember, practice, patience, loving kindness and consistency are what good training is all about.

CHAPTER 8

FINDING A TRAINER WHO'S RIGHT FOR YOU AND YOUR DOG

In this chapter I am going to teach you ways to find, screen and work with professional obedience trainers. While it would be great after reading this book for you and your dog to have no need for a trainer, experience tells me otherwise.

The simple fact is some of the solutions I outline in this book won't work for some people. Other owners, even those who are 100 percent successful in addressing behavior problems, will likely need professional help to teach their dog obedience around distractions and to work on socialization. Finally, some owners may experience more difficult behavioral challenges, such as aggression, separation anxiety, and so on. These types of problems, especially aggression, must be addressed by a qualified professional trainer.

Unfortunately, finding the right trainer isn't always easy. Where do you find a good trainer? How do you know if a trainer is good? What questions should you ask of a trainer?

As I write this book in 2003, nowhere in the United States are dog obedience trainers tested or licensed. This is also true in all Canadian provinces. By dog obedience trainers, I mean those people who teach companion or pet dog obedience. (I am not talking about trainers who teach dogs to sniff bombs, work at search and rescue or with police dogs. Nor am I talking about service dog trainers.) To put it another way, anyone who wants to call themselves a pet dog trainer can do so. You can print up business cards, hand them out, set up an answering machine for your new training business and—poof!—you're a dog trainer. That's kind of scary, when you think about it.

Because there are no state or federal standards for dog trainers, it is up to dog owners to make educated choices about whom to hire.

Regardless of which trainer you choose and which training methods and/or principles they subscribe to, there are really only three basic kinds of programs trainers offer:

1. Group obedience training

2. Private obedience training

3. In-kennel training

GROUP OBEDIENCE TRAINING

Group training involves you taking your dog to a place where there are four to 20 other like-minded people and their dogs. At this location, a trainer will teach everyone how to train their pets. In most basic classes, commands are taught entirely while the dog is on a leash. Basic commands are usually sit, stay, come, down, heel and loose leash walking. Aside from obedience, simple problem-solving instructions to help owners address jumping, chewing, digging and housebreaking are usually included.

FYI, "heel" means the dog walks directly at your left side with his front legs even with yours while remaining completely focused on you at all times, regardless of distractions. In the old days, a lot of time was spent teaching this command. The only problem with "heel" is that most people only need their dogs to walk in this way maybe 5 to 20 percent of the time—for example, when you're on a walk and you approach another dog or when you're walking in a crowded area. Over the last decade or so, a more relaxed form of walking your dog, often called "loose leash walking," has become popular. When you hear this term, understand it means you can walk your dog on your left side without expecting total focus or perfect body placement (unlike heeling). The dog can relax and enjoy the walk, as long as he doesn't pull you.

Some classes have more than one trainer, thus ensuring a lower trainer-to-student ratio. Some classes are indoors and others are outdoors.

Group class training is usually the least expensive. Many class programs are purchased as a series, for example, seven weeks, once a week, for $89. A few programs offer the option of paying for sessions as you go, for example, $7 per lesson. I have seen classes where students were expected to come twice a week. One nationally offered program features a "lifetime" membership where owners can take their dogs back for refresher training as often as they like.

The thing to remember about group obedience training is that it is really *owner* training. You are being trained how to train your dog. For some owners, this might seem somewhat odd. You might ask, "If I'm taking my dog to class so that she learns to sit, why am I the one being trained?" The answer is that in group class, the trainer often will not have the time to individually train each and every dog. And even if the trainer did have the time to begin teaching your dog in class, the dog will need consistent reinforcement throughout the upcoming week. Who's going to do that? The answer is—you!

Besides, you need to ask yourself whether you want a dog who listens to the trainer or a dog who listens to you. Remember, dogs are social animals, meaning they will interact with each person who interacts with them, based on what that individual does or doesn't do. To put it another way, if you take your dog to class each week and, during that class, a trainer using proper training techniques consistently shows your dog what they want the dog to do, your dog will quickly learn to respond to the trainer. If, during the week, you consistently teach your dog not to listen by using the wrong techniques, the end result will be a dog who doesn't listen to you.

The advantages of group obedience training are:

◆ **Price.**

◆ **Your dog learns to follow instructions around distractions.** This is an important benefit. Dogs who respond to commands around people, dogs and other real-world distractions are likely to be much easier and safer to handle in public. This is critical. The first time your dog starts to run across the street to check out a dog on the other side, you will understand the importance of consistent response around distractions.

◆ **Socialization.** This is also an important benefit. Some dogs don't get the opportunity to be around people and other dogs. This can present a real problem for some dogs, especially if they don't learn to properly interact with people and other dogs before they are five months old. There are critical social skills of interaction that every dog must learn. I have seen dogs who are extremely uncomfortable, nervous, jumpy, unpredictable and unsafe around strangers and dogs just because they weren't properly socialized. When a dog learns to be comfortable interacting with people and dogs, you can safely say this dog is well socialized.

The disadvantages of group obedience training are:

◆ **Lack of individual attention.** Some owners and their dogs require a little more one-on-one training and attention to master the skills necessary to succeed.

◆ **Some behavior problems that occur at home can be more difficult to solve in a group class,** where those problems don't arise. For example, an owner with a housebreaking problem whose dog doesn't respond to the general solution guidelines typically given in a group class may require more attention than a group class can offer. In these cases, the trainer may need to visit the home and speak with everyone who interacts with the dog.

◆ **Inconvenience.** A group class is scheduled at a set time, which might not work with your schedule. Additionally, if you miss a class, you might have to wait several weeks before you can make up that class.

PRIVATE OBEDIENCE TRAINING

This type of program usually involves a trainer working with you and your dog one-on-one. Most private lessons take place in your home, although some can be conducted at other places you frequent and where you expect your dog to obey.

Obedience commands can be customized to fit your needs, although typically the basics need to be covered. These include sit, stay, come, down, heel and loose leash walking. Problem solving, including environmentally specific requests and more difficult behavioral challenges, are typically addressed in this kind of program. For example, if you want to teach your dog not to run out your front gate, the trainer can work with you and your dog right at your gate, increasing the likelihood of success.

Many private pet trainers give owners the option of paying for lessons one at a time. Prices can vary depending on your region and the trainer's reputation and experience. Typical price ranges in 2003 are $25 to $150 per session. Some trainers charge more. Some trainers charge by the hour and others by the lesson. This is an important point and one owners should be aware of. If a trainer charges $75 per hour and each lesson takes two hours, that's $150 per lesson. Other trainers charge by the lesson, meaning a flat fee regardless of how long the lesson lasts. Personally, I prefer the latter if the price is reasonable.

There are trainers who also offer programs such as a four-week or seven-week program for a flat fee. Usually purchasing a series of lessons will offer some savings over the same number of lessons purchased separately. For example, lessons may be $75 each or four for $250.

Private lesson pet training is also *owner* training. However, some private trainers will teach your dog obedience commands and then teach you how to handle an already trained dog. This can be an advantage for some owners, *provided you understand that the trainer can't do it all for you.* This is an absolutely critical point. I have met hundreds of owners who have spent thousands of dollars apiece with trainers before they learned this lesson. Most owners speak a different language than trainers. What a trainer says isn't always what an owner hears, and vice versa. A typical scenario sounds like this:

Owner: I want my dog to be trained.

Trainer: What would you like your dog to learn?

Owner: I need him to listen. You know, come when I call him, not to chew my couch, stop jumping all over people, not drag me down the street and stop having accidents in the house.

Trainer: We can work on all of that.

Owner: Great!

While the dialogue here is simple, most owners don't realize that they are really asking for two different things.

The first is problem solving. Chewing the couch, jumping all over people, having accidents in the house all fall into this category. But the simple fact is, no trainer coming to your home is going to be able to housebreak your dog for you—not unless they move in! This means you, the owner, will have to learn the necessary techniques so that you can housebreak the dog, address his chewing and jumping and deal with any other canine problems.

The second is obedience. Coming when called and not dragging you down the street on a walk fall into this category. A trainer could teach your dog to come when *they* call and certainly to not drag *them* down the street. However, only *you* will be able to teach your dog to listen to *you.*

Many trainers say that obedience (sit, stay, come, heel, etc.) is related to problem solving, and that if your dog doesn't listen to simple commands, teaching him to stop engaging in problem behaviors is difficult or impossible. This is not always true. For example, your dog doesn't need to know a single command in order to learn to stop chewing on your couch or to be housebroken. That being said, obedience is important, because it enables you to build a stronger relationship with your dog. It also can be used to address many (but not all) problems.

One thing to be careful about when looking at different programs is the "guarantees." Some trainers claim that their training programs are "guaranteed." I don't usually see "guarantees" offered in group training, but some private and in-kennel programs make these claims. As an owner, I would be extremely skeptical about "guarantees" or any trainer who offers them.

I remember meeting with owners who had spent $1,500 with a trainer. The owners originally contacted the trainer because their six-month-old Great Dane was not housebroken. The dog also jumped all over people in a friendly, Marmaduke fashion. Finally, the owners recognized that their dog really did need to listen to some basic commands.

The trainer came to their house, heard their request and signed them up for a training program. In this program, the trainer was to work with the dog three times a week for several months, teaching obedience. According to the owners, when they asked about housebreaking, the trainer said that "solutions will be given." Included in the contract was a written "guarantee" stating "if your dog regresses from any of the commands I teach during the training program, I will retrain the dog at no additional cost."

The problem was that the "guarantee" was irrelevant. When the dog didn't listen to the owners and was still not housebroken, they called the trainer. This trainer went back to their home, reviewed the obedience commands he had taught the dog, and, since he had trained the dog in the first place, the dog was perfectly responsive to him. The trainer then said the dog had not regressed from any of the commands he taught and there was nothing else he could do! When the owners asked about housebreaking, the trainer responded that he had given the owners written material on the subject.

The owners thought housebreaking, chewing and obedience were "guaranteed," and that the trainer would solve these problems for them. In reality such "guarantees" are really not possible. The bottom line is that it is critical to find someone who is ethical enough to be honest with you.

Here's the truth: *You, the owner, need to learn how to properly communicate with and teach your dog.* This includes simple commands such as come, sit, stay, down, heel and loose leash walking. It also may include you learning various ways of eliminating, redirecting, and/or curtailing behavior problems. If you expect your dog to learn these skills, you will need to spend time every day working with your dog. You will need to do this for at least four to eight months. Some dogs may require less time; many will require more. The only shortcut is for you to be consistent and use effective, humane training techniques.

Trainers who are willing to tell you something similar to what I have just said are the ones I would consider hiring.

The advantages of private lessons are:

◆ **Individual attention.** Most private lessons are one-on-one and offer a great deal of individual attention with the trainer.

◆ **Environmentally specific problems.** Problems that only occur at home are most effectively addressed in the environment they take place in.

◆ **Convenience.** Lessons can be set up around your schedule. It is also sometimes easier for several family members to all be home at the same time, as opposed to everyone going to a group class or kennel at the same time.

◆ **Customized training.** Because of the individual attention and the fact that the dog is being trained in his actual environment, custom training can often be more effective using private lessons.

The disadvantages of private lessons are:

◆ **Price.** Private lessons can run from several hundred to several thousand dollars.

◆ **No socialization.** While it is important for dogs to learn to behave where they live, it is also critical for dogs to be exposed to other people and animals. If private lessons are *only* conducted in your home, critical socialization opportunities may be missed.

- **Fewer distractions.** Here too, while it is important for your dog to obey at home, it is also important for your dog to obey in public. If private lessons are *only* conducted in your home, your dog may not get the necessary work around distractions he needs to be responsive to commands in most real-world situations.

IN-KENNEL TRAINING

These programs typically require you to board your dog at a kennel for a specific length of time, during which the dog is trained at the kennel by a professional trainer. Most kennel programs teach obedience basics. Programs can vary in length from a week to several months.

This type of training is normally the most expensive, and can run from several hundred dollars to many thousands. In-kennel obedience programs have an advantage over group or private lessons, because there is no owner inconsistency to interfere with the training. Several weeks or months of consistent training can really make a difference, and dogs can be fantastically well trained in this environment. However, they will be fantastically well trained and listen to the professional trainer! You still need to learn how to get the same response from your dog. When you're researching a kennel program, make sure handling lessons for dog owners are included in the course so that you get the necessary training on how to handle your already trained dog.

Many owners ask, "If my dog is professionally trained and I can see he really listens to the trainer, won't it be easier at that point to get the dog to listen to me?"

The answer is, it really depends. True, the dog has learned to listen to the trainer, but most dogs have already learned *not* to listen to their owners. Not listening to you isn't usually something your dog forgets. The bottom line is that most owners need to be prepared to spend months reinforcing the fact that their dog needs to respond to them. Additionally, remember that problem behaviors, such as chewing, digging, jumping, nipping, housebreaking, barking, door crashing, etc., *must* be addressed by the owner, in the home.

One variation on the kennel theme involves leaving your dog at the kennel during the day for training and socialization and picking the dog up at night. This is an interesting and potentially effective way to train, although ultimately there is no getting around the fact that you, the owner, are going to have to learn how to get your dog to listen to you.

Problem solving can be a little bit more difficult in kennel training programs. The reason is relatively simple: If your dog is digging huge holes in your yard, how is sending the dog to a kennel for a month (where there's no yard) going to solve this problem? It won't, and those owners who spend $1,000 in the hopes it will are likely to be very disappointed.

Some problems of a more advanced nature, for example certain types of aggression, can be addressed in-kennel. Extremely fearful dogs can be successfully worked with in this environment, because skilled professionals taking advantage of a very consistent, controlled environment can modify more difficult behaviors.

For some owners, especially those with discretionary income, in-kennel training is an excellent option, especially if they're boarding their dogs when they're going on vacation. If you're leaving for a month, why not have your dog learn some basic commands? There is certainly nothing wrong with this idea, provided you are very clear about the work you need to do with your dog when you get back.

The advantages of in-kennel training are:

◆ **Convenience.** The dog is trained in a consistent environment and the owners don't have to be involved until the behaviors are already learned.

◆ **Consistency.** Since the owners are not involved in the initial training process, the dog can be trained more consistently and sometimes more effectively.

◆ **Some difficult problems can be more effectively addressed in a kennel.** Most cannot.

The disadvantages of in-kennel training are:

◆ **Price.** Kennel training is usually the most expensive.

◆ **Relevance.** Most owners need to address behavioral challenges at home. Kennel training is not the most effective way to deal with common in-home problems.

I have trained dogs using all three types of programs. I recognize that each has strengths and weaknesses. You need to assess exactly what you want to accomplish and, very critically, whether you are prepared to commit the time to get the response you're after. In my experience, group class training is an excellent option and so is private training with group class as a follow-up. In-kennel training with a group class follow-up can also be very effective. What would I do? Assuming my dog had common problems, such as housebreaking, chewing and jumping, and I needed to teach him basic commands, I would probably take one to five private lessons to address home concerns and then get my dog into group class to strengthen obedience around distractions and to work on socialization.

HOW TO FIND A TRAINER

Now that I've reviewed the different programs, let's discuss how to find a trainer. I would look for the following things.

Reputation

You want someone with an excellent reputation. The first person I would ask is my dog's veterinarian. In my experience, a veterinary referral is the best place to start, because veterinarians are likely to give you an objective opinion based on client feedback without an agenda. What do I mean by this? Vets aren't trainers. They're not competing and have nothing to gain by referring or not referring an obedience trainer.

I wouldn't just take a card or brochure from my vet's office—I would ask the vet and front office staff about this trainer. Often, the front office hears a tremendous amount of client feedback. Sometimes even more than the doctor. Has this trainer worked with other clients? What was the feedback?

Assuming I got answers that worked for me, I would probably check with another veterinarian in my area as well. You don't have to be a client there. A simple phone call or a 10-minute visit will usually get you all the information you need. You might wind up with two good referrals for two trainers, or the same trainer might be recommended at both offices.

If you don't find who you're looking for at your vet's office, you can also speak to employees at pet supply stores and professional groomers. Both of these groups work extensively with dog owners and have many opportunities to hear the good, bad and ugly things about local trainers.

By the way, I don't want anyone reading this to get the idea that most trainers are bad. Nothing could be further from the truth. Most trainers are true animal lovers who are thrilled that they can actually get paid to train and be with dogs. However, since knowledge and skill vary so greatly, it is absolutely imperative that you find the right trainer for you.

Some pet supply stores offer training right at their facilities. This is worth looking into, and it will be very easy to observe training classes and ask customers and store employees for feedback about them. These classes can be convenient and have an added benefit that all your training equipment is available right where the class is being taught.

Aside from veterinarians, pet supply stores and groomers, I strongly recommend you speak with the people in your life—friends and family. Have any of your friends worked with dog trainers? If yes, with whom? What was the outcome? Did they like the trainer? If yes, why? If no, why not?

The First Call

Once you've gotten a few names, call these trainers. If the trainer isn't there, leave a message and note when you called. Trainers should respond in at least 24 hours, maybe 48 if you call on a weekend.

Trainers who can't get back with you in two days are likely too busy, and I would probably eliminate them from consideration. You might think, "If they're busy, maybe that's because they're really good." This might be a valid point, but if they're so busy they can't call you back quickly, how will it be if you need them during the training program?

Once the trainer calls you back (in a timely fashion), you can start to interact with them and ask questions. Most trainers will need to get some basic information about you and your pet. Dog breed, age, sex, spayed/neutered, problems, your goals are all fair questions. I would eliminate any trainers who want to know anything about your income level.

Once you've given the trainer some basic data, the trainer should explain to you what type of programs they offer: Group classes? Private lessons? In-kennel training? Some? All? If the trainer offers group or kennel training, ask if you can visit a class or the kennel to watch the trainer work. Trainers who refuse should be eliminated. I would also ask how much experience the trainer has, who they trained under and what their basic training philosophy is all about. Does this trainer offer "guarantees" (see page 165) or are they pretty up-front about you having to do the work if you expect your dog to respond to you?

While it is not reasonable to expect a trainer to spend hours on the phone with potential clients (some will), it is also fair to expect a 10- to 15-minute conversation in which you get the answers to the questions I've just listed. If you're not comfortable with the trainer's communication style or responses, ask yourself whether this is a person you would feel comfortable working with. If the answer is no, eliminate this trainer and move on.

References

Ask the trainer for references, specifically the names and numbers of clients they have worked with. I would ask for two or three. Trainers who are unwilling to supply them should be eliminated from consideration. That being said, I have never felt that asking someone for a reference will automatically give me an accurate indication of this person's ability or professionalism. Maybe I'm just cynical (a little), but I always think, "Is this person really going to give me the name of a dissatisfied customer?" Still, I would ask and probably call one or two of the references, just to hear what they have to say.

Observation

When observing a group class, watch the way the trainer interacts with their students. Do they yell and browbeat students? Do they only have one way of explaining the same concept? How does the trainer interact with the dogs? Are they gentle, patient and obviously concerned? Is the trainer articulate? Do they teach in a way that is easy for you, an observer, to understand? Chances are if you can't understand much of what a trainer is saying to the class, and most of the people seem pretty confused as well, it's probably a good idea to look elsewhere. But be reasonable. Students who are attending week one of a seven-week obedience class are likely to be a bit confused. How quickly does the trainer sort this out?

Is the trainer rough? Are they recommending the same equipment for every single dog? For example, choke chains for a timid five-month-old Cocker Spaniel and a rambunctious eight-month-old Rottweiler? Generally, trainers who only use one type of equipment or train using one method will not be as effective as those who are open to a variety of techniques that are based on each individual owner's and dog's needs and temperament.

Another thing to look for is trainer-to-student ratio. Depending on their experience, some trainers can handle larger classes. But in my experience, more than 15 dogs per trainer is too much. Again, every trainer is different and there are undoubtedly instructors out there who can easily handle 20 dogs. But generally, if a class has more than 15, look for two trainers or at least one trainer and an assistant. By assistant I'm talking about an apprentice, someone learning to be a trainer.

Also, look at the way the class is run. Does the trainer spend 10 minutes with each student while everyone else stands around? In bigger classes this is not an effective way to train. Does the trainer give the class a lot of group exercises and then work briefly with each student while the rest of the class is engaged in the exercises? This style can often result in a fair amount of individual attention for all students, while at the same time ensuring there is very little stand-around time. With bigger classes of 10 or more dogs, this is important.

As an observer, you need to be careful not to interfere. However, it is reasonable to speak with students after class. Did they like the class? If so, why? If not, why? Feedback like this can be invaluable.

When observing group classes, if possible, try to see at least two. Ideally, visit a first- or second-week class to see how well the trainer handles the pandemonium of a new class, and graduation to see how well the dogs have progressed. It's not necessary to wait to see graduation of the same class you observed at week one or two. All you're really looking for is an indication of how much dogs and owners learn in this trainer's classes.

Graduation

It's also worth knowing how many people graduated the class, compared to how many started it. A good trainer will know their graduation rate. Do 50 percent of the students graduate? 80 percent? 10 percent? Trainers who don't have a clue should probably be eliminated from consideration. They may not know the exact percentage, but if they don't have an idea, it might be an indication that they don't care. You are looking for trainers with a high percentage of students who started the program going all the way through to graduation. Sixty to 80 percent is a reasonable rate, but again, try to be fair. Sometimes some classes just don't do well. Different times of the year, especially around the holidays, can cause graduation rates to fluctuate. I would not base my decision just on graduation rates, but it's worth knowing.

During graduation, does the trainer encourage all the students? Is the graduation a positive event, or does the trainer spend most of the time telling the students they could have done better? Does the trainer give out diplomas? Trophies? Dog biscuits? Little gifts at the end of class do not mean you are looking at a good trainer. However, often trainers who are willing to spend a little extra time and money to give students just a little bit more are trainers who take their job more seriously.

Programs

Does the trainer offer more advanced programs? Do they just teach basic classes? What if you want to go on to the next level? How about puppy training? Does the trainer offer special classes for that? Even if you're only interested in basic obedience, trainers who are capable of teaching several levels of obedience are often more well-rounded instructors with a greater depth of knowledge.

Puppy classes, sometimes called Puppy Kindergarten, are usually designed for puppies up to five months of age. Puppy classes usually focus on socialization, some very simple obedience, and common behavior problems. Most are not that much different from basic classes, and should be thought of as a foundation or introduction to basic obedience. I recommend them.

The requirements to enter puppy classes will vary, and it is best to check with your veterinarian about when you can safely take your puppy to a class. Some very nasty diseases, such as parvovirus and distemper (both of which can be fatal) can be contracted by puppies who have not been fully inoculated.

Intermediate or advanced classes can mean many different things, depending on the trainer. Most intermediate classes involve sharpening already learned basic commands around more difficult distractions and working toward obtaining off-leash control. Advanced classes can involve off-leash obedience, as well as a variety of other skills. These include jumping over hurdles, scent discrimination exercises and others. You may have no interest when you first start classes in going through to an advanced level. But it's still good to know your trainer can take you there, if you desire. It's also possible that you will follow in the footsteps of millions of dog owners and discover, to your surprise, that you genuinely *like* training your dog. What initially starts as a chore can often become a real labor of love.

If you're observing a trainer teaching in-kennel, it's important to see them work with dogs who are at different levels in the training process. See how the trainer works with a beginning dog. See how they work with a dog whose training is almost complete. It's also important to make sure the trainer you're hiring is the trainer who is actually doing the teaching in the kennel. I've known trainers who primarily promoted their business and hired others to do the training. While there is absolutely nothing wrong with this, it's only fair that you observe the actual trainer who would work with you and your pet before you decide whether to hire this person. Remember to also observe kennel trainers when they are teaching the owners how to handle their already trained dogs. It will do you very little good to hire a trainer who is gifted in teaching dogs, but who has little or no ability to teach you to do the same. This is an important point.

People Skills

Some trainers are outstanding at training dogs, but have little or no people skills. Trainers like this will be very difficult to learn from. Some trainers are great communicators but don't do a whole lot of actual training. They're better at talking than actually training. You are looking for a combination of both: a trainer who is good with the dogs, yet is also comfortable enough around people to express themselves in a way that enables dogs and humans both to learn and grow from the training experience.

More Questions

After you have observed the trainer in action, spoken to some of the students, received good recommendations about this trainer from friends, family, vets, groomers or pet supply stores, it's a good idea to ask a few other questions.

Ask to see the trainer's own dog work. As surprising as it sounds, not all trainers have fantastically trained dogs of their own. However, a trainer who believes in what they teach and has applied it to their own dog is someone I would be more interested in working with.

Ask the trainer who they were taught by. Also ask what their opinion of this trainer is now. Many trainers learn their skills by working with other trainers. If a trainer is self-taught, they may lack a certain depth of knowledge. Ideally, a trainer will have worked with a few other professionals, so they are more well-rounded.

Listening to the opinions trainers have of other trainers can tell you a lot about their personality. Training is an inexact science. This is certainly true in the real world. With hundreds of dog breeds, unlimited numbers of mixed breeds, every conceivable owner temperament and environmental differences as varied as you can imagine, there is no one method that will work in every situation. Trainers who bad-mouth fellow instructors because they disagree with their methods are often showing their own rigidity and narrow-mindedness. This isn't always the case, and some trainers really do deserve bad reputations. However, if you speak to a trainer whose favorite instructor is him- /herself, and this person has nothing good to say about anyone else, I would steer clear.

Ask what training magazines and books they have read in the last year. Like I've said before, be fair. It is simply not possible to read the huge amount of material published each year on this subject. There's a lot more available than there is time to read it. However, trainers who don't read anything are probably not as interested in keeping up on the subject of canine behavior and training. How involved and interested are they if they don't make a little time for continuing education?

Ask if they belong to any dog trainer organizations. As I write this book, there are three national organizations that focus on pet dog trainers and one whose members specialize in more advanced training.

The first group is the International Association of Canine Professionals (IACP). This group is open to all trainers, but has rigid standards for admission. Letters of referral from fellow professionals and minimum experience requirements come into play when determining whether a trainer is admitted as an Affiliate, Associate or Professional. A Professional member must have five years of professional training experience, an Associate up to five years.

This group is extremely open-minded regarding training philosophies, and as such its members use many different training methods. Personally, I think this is a good thing, because it gives you more choices when choosing a trainer. And, as I mentioned earlier in this book, that is definitely an advantage, because trainers who only use one method of training often limit themselves and their effectiveness.

The IACP also offers testing and certification. There is a written test, and the trainer must also submit a videotape demonstrating their training ability.

The largest group is the Association of Pet Dog Trainers (APDT). This group is open to "anyone who teaches people to train their dogs." A full membership in this group costs $75 and the prerequisites for joining are paying the membership fee.

The APDT has developed certain guidelines for training and a certification program for pet dog trainers, and now a certification council called the Certification Council for Pet Dog Trainers (CCPDT) offers testing. The CCPDT is a separate body from the APDT and is responsible for certification testing. The test is difficult, and only trainers with 300 hours of dog training experience will be admitted for examination. This test is a written multiple choice exam with roughly 250 questions that gauge a trainer's theoretical understanding of learning theory, training equipment, animal husbandry, ethology (animal behavior) and instruction skills. Trainers who pass the CCPDT's written test can call themselves certified pet dog trainers (CPDT).

The third group is called the National Association of Dog Obedience Instructors (NADOI). This is the oldest of the trainer organizations and also the most difficult for trainers to join. Trainers have to fulfill very specific standards to become members. According to NADOI, applicants must have at least five years' experience in dog obedience training, including two years as a full charge instructor (they have full responsibility for a class). They must have worked with a minimum of 100 dogs. Group instructors must have taught at least 104 class hours, and private instructors, 288 hours. Applicants are required to take a written test, and NADOI reserves the right to conduct personal interviews and observation, as well as request a videotape from the applicant showing their training skills. This is an excellent organization.

I would not eliminate a trainer just because they aren't a member of one of these groups. However, I would consider membership in the IACP or NADOI a plus, because it shows that certain standards were met. I would also consider certification from any of these groups to be a plus. (For information on these trainer organizations, as well as other resources you may use to locate a trainer near you, check out Chapter 9, Have Fun: Resources for You and Your Dog.)

With any luck, you and your dog can have a relationship for 10 or 15 or maybe even 17 years. That's a long time. It's an important relationship, and one that can give both of you tremendous rewards. Training strengthens the bond between you and your dog. It teaches you better ways to communicate with your pet and enables your pet to safely learn from you. By the way, as crazy as it might sound, you will also learn a great many things from your dog. These include patience, understanding, respect and, hopefully, unconditional love. It is worth spending three or four hours doing the research and observing trainers at work so that you can choose a trainer who can most effectively assist you. In the end, you may just have to go with your gut feelings. And you must remember that a training program is only as good as the amount of time, effort and desire *you* put into it.

CHAPTER 9

HAVE FUN: RESOURCES FOR YOU AND YOUR DOG

We live in an amazing time. The Internet is a phenomenal resource that contains information on just about anything. Information about dogs is readily available if you know where to look. When you're checking out various Internet sites, remember to make a note about other sites that are connected to the original site you're looking at. Using this technique, you can quickly locate as many sites as you need on a given topic and on related topics. The key is to write them down.

This chapter will focus on specific canine categories. I will refer to sites that I have seen and give a quick synopsis of my thoughts and feelings about what I found on the site. You may have a different view, but I strongly recommend you check them out. Have fun surfing doggie style.

For those people interested in becoming professional trainers themselves, there's even a reference guide listing schools and various educational options to help you get started.

BEHAVIOR

There are dozens of Internet sites that focus on canine behavior. However, many of them are written for professionals. This doesn't help the average dog owner. Luckily, there are a few excellent ones for laypeople.

Dr. P's Dog Training, www.uwsp.edu/psych/dog/dog.htm

This is an extremely comprehensive site. Dr. Mark Plonsky (Dr. P) is a psychology professor and has compiled a tremendous amount of behavioral information. To find articles and advice about behavior, go to the site and click on the library or your topic of choice: puppies, housebreaking or some other specific issue. There are also articles on obedience, protection, military training, a variety of dog sports, e-lists enabling you to connect with other people and much more. You can spend hours and hours on this site.

What You Need to Know About Dogs, dogs.about.com/index.htm

This is also a very comprehensive site. You also have options that enable you to link to numerous other sites. For example, there's a detailed A-to-Z index of dog rescue organizations, information on breeders, breeds, training, behavior issues and much more. You can spend hours on this site as well, and days following the hundreds of links.

Petco Animal Supplies, www.Petco.com

Petco has excellent information about canine behavior on their site. Go to their home page and click on "Tips and Talk, Learn about Pets." This will take you to the portion of the site devoted to behavior. You can choose from various problems and get tips on how to address them.

LOCATING TRAINERS

International Association of Canine Professionals (IACP), www.dogpro.org

This is one of several organizations of professional pet dog trainers. The IACP also offers affiliate memberships for people who are not trainers. Go to their home page, click on "membership," and then along the left-hand side of the page, click on "members list." All trainers in the IACP are listed, with contact information.

Association of Pet Dog Trainers (APDT), www.apdt.com

This is the largest of the trainer organizations. With several thousand members, the APDT has a large database of professional trainers. To find them, go to the home page, click on "trainers and owners," then click on "trainer search," then "trainer directory." Enter your state and start your search.

National Association of Dog Obedience Instructors (NADOI), www.nadoi.org

NADOI is the oldest of the trainer organizations, and the most difficult for trainers to join. To find trainers, go to the home page, click on "find instructors" and follow the prompts.

American Kennel Club (AKC), www.akc.org

The American Kennel Club has an extensive site, which includes information on obedience clubs recognized by the AKC. Obedience clubs that are affiliated with the AKC usually focus on helping people train their dogs to compete in obedience trials (which are only open to AKC-registered dogs). However, many clubs will allow mixed breed dogs in their classes. If you'd like to observe classes in your area, obedience clubs can give you an excellent opportunity to do just that. To find a club nearest you, go to the AKC home page, click on "clubs" and then "club search." Then click on "obedience clubs." Once you're there, follow the prompts.

These four sites will give you a very wide range of trainers and training styles. Remember to review Chapter 8 for information on how to screen obedience trainers. Also don't forget the importance of personal and professional referrals.

Here's an extra site to check out: **www.clickertraining.com.** This site belongs to Karen Pryor, a renowned author and lecturer. She has written many books, including *Don't Shoot the Dog,* which is considered by some to be one of the best books on behavior ever written.

Karen Pryor is arguably the greatest clicker training expert in the world, and her site contains a wealth of information about behavior, clicker training and where to find clicker trainers. Check it out.

DOG PARKS

In urban areas, dog parks are becoming more and more popular. These are places owners and their dogs can go for a little off-leash play and socialization. A few words of advice regarding these parks: Before taking your dog to one, go to it yourself a few times. Most dog parks attract people who are genuinely interested in congregating with friendly, sociable dogs. The parks are clean and properly fenced. However, there are some that attract a less savory element. Believe it or not, there are some people who knowingly bring their dog-aggressive pets to a park because they think it's amusing to watch their dogs bullying other dogs. If you have the misfortune to observe a park that attracts such pinheads, steer clear. I detest bullies and make it a point to tip off animal control if I believe parks near me are having problems with people of this type. That being said, most dog parks are really a kick for people and their pets. By the way, for all you singles, the doggie park is often a very interesting social scene.

To find a park nearest you, go to **www.dogpark.com/dpark.html.** Click on "dog parks in the U.S." (unless, of course, you live in Canada, in which case click on "dog parks in Canada"). Once you're there, follow the prompts. There's also good information on dog park etiquette that's worth reading.

BOARDING KENNELS

If you're looking for a place to board your dog, where do you go? You can certainly ask for a referral from your veterinarian, but a word of caution: Some veterinary hospitals also offer boarding. Unfortunately, some of these hospitals aren't really set up as boarding kennels. To find a certified boarding kennel, I recommend you visit the American Boarding Kennel's (ABKA) Web site at **www.abka.com.** The ABKA has an excellent site and takes the business of kenneling very seriously. ABKA members are serious about their profession. To find a member kennel, go to the home page and click on "member kennels." Follow the prompts from there. The ABKA site also has a lot of other information, and is definitely worth checking out even if you are not looking for a kennel.

PET-FRIENDLY LOCATIONS

www.petswelcome.com

If you're looking for a hotel, motel, campground, apartment, bed and breakfast, amusement park, even ski resorts that accept pets, this site is awesome. I was very surprised at some of the high-end hotels throughout the country that will accept dogs. Looking to relocate? Find your apartment here. You can even find a ski resort. This is a great resource.

www.dogfriendly.com

This site also lists dog-friendly places, although much of the information is in the form of guides and pet travel books that are for sale. Still, it's worth checking out.

VETERINARIANS

www.vetlocator.petplace.com

Often new dog owners have no idea where to find a veterinarian. Vetlocator makes this task much easier. Simply click on the home page, enter your Zip code (or in Canada, your postal code), list the distance you're willing to travel, and you will find vets in your area. The site doesn't endorse specific veterinarians, it simply lists them. There are also some interesting articles on behavior, medicine, veterinary insurance and other animals, as well. A very worthwhile and easy-to-use Web site.

CANINE READING

When I started training, the only books on canine behavior I could find were old ones at the local library and a few at the local book store.

While there are larger selections available at large book chains, such as Barnes & Noble and Borders, some training guides are very specialized and are difficult to find. A good place to find many hard-to-find titles is **www.dogwise.com.** I also recommend **www.amazon.com,** because you can find just about anything on this site.

I mentioned dog magazines earlier in the book. The three I mentioned all have Web sites.

DogWorld, which is primarily devoted to people who are competing in organized dog sports, is still worth reading. A lot of breeders advertise in this magazine, and *DogWorld* features behavior articles. Check them out at **www.dogworldmag.com.** *DogWorld* is sold at many major bookstores.

Dog Fancy is devoted to pet dog lovers and has more training articles. It's a good magazine for all-around dog knowledge and I highly recommend it. Check it out at **www.dogfancy.com.** *Dog Fancy* is sold at many major bookstores.

Off Lead magazine is written for professional dog trainers and serious obedience competitors. The articles can be a bit more difficult, but are well worth reading. This is a smaller publication and can only be purchased via subscription. Check out *Off Lead* magazine at **www.barkleigh.com.** When you go to the site, click on "Off Lead," which is found on the left of the page.

LEGAL ISSUES

Dog owners are sometimes faced with bewildering legal questions. What happens if your dog bites someone or runs out in the street and causes a traffic accident? What are you responsible for? While all owners should talk to a lawyer who is familiar with the laws of their specific state and province, **www.dogbitelaw.com,** a Web site hosted by lawyer Kenneth Phillips is an excellent place to go. It's extensive and answers numerous questions. Considering that dog bites cause financial losses exceeding $1 billion every year, some information is a very good idea. The site also features most commonly asked questions, lots of links and the opportunity to e-mail Kenneth Phillips for practical information about dog bite issues.

PET PRODUCTS

For those of you who like shopping on line, check out Petco's Web site at **www.Petco.com.** They have thousands and thousands of items to choose from.

SCHOOLS FOR DOG TRAINERS

If you are interested in becoming a professional dog trainer, check out these schools.

Triple Crown Academy
200 CR 197
Hutto, TX 78634
www.triplecrowndogs.com

Arizona Canine
P.O. Box 1936
Sierra Vista, AZ 85636
877-K9-ACADEMY
www.azcanine.com

West Virginia Canine College
P.O. Box 2078
Buckhannon, WV 26201
304-472-6691
www1.neumedia.net or e-mail: info@wvcc.com

The Tom Rose School
6701 Antire Rd.
High Ridge, MO 63049
888-TOM-ROSE
www.tomrose.com or e-mail: tomrose@oui.com

Animal Behavior College
9018 Balboa Blvd., #591
Northridge, CA 91325
800-801-6239
www.animalbehaviorcollege.com

OTHER DOG SITES

www.petfinder.org
If you're looking to adopt a dog, check out this site. You'll find hundreds of animal shelters throughout North America with pets waiting for good homes.

www.hsus.org
The Humane Society of the United States (HSUS) is an organization dedicated to the welfare of animals. It's not just about dogs. This is an interesting site.

www.petsit.com
Pet Sitters International is an organization for professional pet sitters. More and more people are choosing to leave their dogs at home under the care of a pet sitter instead of boarding their dog in a kennel. This site is about pet sitters and has a search feature that enables you to find a pet sitter near your home.

I hope these Web sites, like this book, will make your life and your dog's life more rewarding. As I said at the beginning of this book, I hope all of you have found this material as fun and rewarding to read as it was to write. If so, I will consider my efforts a smashing success. Good luck to all of you, and give your puppies a kiss from Steve.

SO YOU WANT TO BE A PROFESSIONAL DOG TRAINER

For some people, becoming a professional dog trainer is a lifelong dream. For others, it's an excellent and rewarding part-time job. As I mentioned in Chapter 8, millions of dog owners find, sometimes to their surprise, that they genuinely enjoy training their dogs. They start off at the basic level and gradually teach their dogs to be more proficient in obedience. As they teach their dogs, they are learning themselves, and after a year or two or five they realize that they know an awful lot. Perhaps they've helped a few friends train their dogs. Perhaps they're the resident "expert" that friends and family turn to when asking about all things canine.

When people reach this level, some are perfectly content to remain there. Others might ask themselves, "Why not do something I love (train dogs), and get paid for it at the same time?" One of the top trainers in the country and a vice president in my organization got her start after training her dog in 4H.

Regardless of what your motivation is, consider carefully whether you want to go down this path. If you decide to, good luck. And who knows, I may just meet you at a training event!

Types of Training Programs

Professional trainers can offer many types of training programs. These programs usually address two main subjects. The first subject is problem solving and the second is basic obedience. Aside from the basics, professional trainers often offer more advanced treatment programs for difficult behaviors. These include separation anxiety (dogs who can't tolerate being left alone), phobias and aggression. Not all professional trainers are qualified to address these problems, and there is a great need for professionals who can offer counseling and treatment programs to address these serious behaviors.

Some trainers make a living teaching dogs to perform in movies and on television. It can take many years for someone to attain the knowledge and experience needed to train in this specialized field. If your goal is to become a motion picture trainer or to specialize in more complex behavior problems, you must first break into the business by mastering the basics.

It is important to understand that while there are endless variations on how the basic subjects can be taught to the public, there are really only three training program options that most trainers offer: group classes, private in-home training and in-kennel training. This was discussed in Chapter 8, so I won't review it here.

Where Do You Start?

At this time, there are no state or federal standards for professional obedience trainers. While trainers who want to conduct business will need to obtain a business license, a business license is for tax purposes and has absolutely no bearing on a trainer's ability. Because there are no recognized government standards, it is critically important for prospective trainers to research all their options before deciding how and where they will obtain their training education.

Apprenticeships

Apprenticeship is a common way for individuals to break into the dog training business. Once a student has successfully completed a class several times, most group trainers will be receptive to the idea of letting them help teach. My company has hired numerous professional trainers who started in the business this way.

To learn this way, find a class you feel comfortable with and take the entire class at least twice. Don't be afraid to ask the trainer questions afterwards. Establish a rapport with the instructor. By the third complete class series, you can probably approach the trainer with an offer to help. It's generally a good idea to offer this assistance free of charge. Most trainers will be more receptive to this approach. Assist for a minimum of three complete class programs. After the third complete class, if you feel you have more to learn from this trainer, continue to assist until your questions are answered or you decide that this trainer has taught you all they can. Try this approach with at least four different trainers. It's a good idea to observe and participate in classes taught using a variety of different training styles. Apprenticeships of this type can take between one and three years.

After a year of consistent observation, participation and assistance in group classes, you can apply for a job at a training kennel. Most training kennels will probably hire you as a kennel helper or assistant, meaning you will likely spend a fair amount of time cleaning and maintaining the facility. You may also have the opportunity to observe and assist in training pets boarded at the kennel. Nothing is more important than training experience, and a boarding kennel is an outstanding environment in which to obtain it.

The apprenticeship approach is a good way to learn the necessary skills to become a professional obedience instructor. The downside is that because this approach lacks a formal educational structure, it may take you months of trial and error to find trainers who can really help you.

Training Schools

There are a number of professional dog trainer schools throughout the United States. Since good training schools offer a precisely focused curriculum designed to teach students exactly what they'll need to become professional trainers, these schools can decrease the amount of time prospective trainers spend studying and apprenticing on their own.

If you are interested in pursuing this option, it's a good idea to get information about the program and a few references from the school's graduates. You should also ask the following questions:

◆ Are the instructors professional trainers themselves? Ideally, the instructors have all taught professionally.

◆ Does the school have a job placement program? This is critical, since most people graduating from a training school do not have the experience to go into business for themselves.

◆ Are the costs competitive?

◆ What types of training methods are taught? A variety of methods should be discussed, including positive reinforcement and compulsion techniques.

◆ Is the instruction all theoretical or is there hands-on training experience as well? *Both hands-on experience and theoretical knowledge are critical.*

There are typically three types of professional training schools. On-campus programs, where you live at the school, usually last between six and 14 weeks. In some instances boarding is included in the price; in others it is extra. It's a good idea to check. Some schools require that you bring a dog, but most will have dogs available to be trained. Cost for these types of programs generally run between $3,500 and $15,000. Here are a few schools you can contact for more information.

Triple Crown Academy
200 CR 197
Hutto, TX 78634
www.triplecrowndogs.com

Arizona Canine
P.O. Box 1936
Sierra Vista, AZ 85636
877-K9-ACADEMY
www.azcanine.com

West Virginia Canine College
P.O. Box 2078
Buckhannon, WV 26201
304-472-6691
www1.neumedia.net

The Tom Rose School
6701 Antire Rd.
High Ridge, MO 63049
888-TOM-ROSE
www.tomrose.com

There are also schools that offer correspondence courses. Some of them are traditional mail order correspondence programs. In these courses, you are sent written material and/or video/audio/CD or DVD materials to study. Some advantages of this type of program are the costs and the fact that you can work at your own pace. While it is certainly possible to learn behavioral theory in this fashion, I recommend you avoid traditional correspondence schools, because professional training involves more than just a theoretical understanding of obedience and behavior. You will also need hands-on experience.

Another variation on the correspondence school theme is the "virtual school." This means that for a fee you can take behavioral classes on the

Internet. Some people might find this more desirable than being mailed materials. However, in my opinion the disadvantages are the same.

Off-campus schools are a relatively new and effective option. They combine the advantage of correspondence (speed and lower cost) with hands-on experience. Off-campus programs can be taken in your community, making attending a dog trainer college a far more realistic option for most people. Additionally, off-campus programs are significantly less expensive than on-campus programs and far more effective than correspondence courses.

To be honest, I am somewhat biased on this subject. I have an off-campus training school that I'm going to list, and I want to be up front with all my readers about this fact. I invite anyone interested to check us out and by all means compare.

Animal Behavior College
9018 Balboa Blvd., #591
Northridge, CA 91325
800-801-6239
www.animalbehaviorcollege.com

The Compensation

Professional dog trainers can work full- or part-time anywhere in the United States. It is an excellent part-time job and requires very little start-up costs to begin your own business. Professional dog trainers can earn at least $20 per hour. Many trainers earn significantly more than that. Full-time trainers can earn $30,000 to $80,000 per year.

Succeeding as a full-time trainer requires building a client base and a referral base. Most successful service businesses get a lot of their business from referrals of satisfied customers. Obviously, it will take several years to have enough satisfied customers to send you anything close to the amount of business you will need to make a living in this profession. I know trainers who have never advertised their business. Not ever! They receive all of their business from referrals of satisfied customers. However, most of these trainers started their businesses as part-time ventures and gradually increased their hours as more business came in.

Aside from a client base, most of you will need to build a referral base. By this I mean a list of pet business contacts that recommend your service. Veterinary hospitals, groomers, pet sitters and pet supply stores fall into this category. When I started my training business in 1980, I built it to full-time in 14 months, relying on referrals. This can be done, but it takes work.

The Rewards

As a trainer, you will be able to have a positive effect on the lives of dozens and possibly hundreds of pet owners and their pets. You will literally be able to save pets' lives. According to Rolan Tripp, DVM, "more dogs die and/or are euthanized due to untreated behavior problems than all preventable diseases combined." Animal shelters across the nation report that anywhere between 20 to 60 percent of the dogs they encounter are there in part because of untreated behavior problems. Among the most common are aggression, house soiling and fence jumping. As a professional trainer, you will help owners address these critical issues to the benefit of all concerned.

Training Books

To help trainers in their quest for knowledge, I recommend the following titles, which cover a variety of training subjects. I have deliberately included a wide range of training philosophies, because I believe every decent student should read as much as they can and be open-minded during the educational process. Form your opinions based on knowledge, not feelings, and you will find that you are a much more well-rounded trainer.

Some training books are difficult to locate, and some are out of print (I have marked those with an *). One outstanding place to locate just about any book you can imagine about training is Dogwise. This is a direct book service and is worth investigating. You can view their selection by visiting them online at **www.dogwise.com.** Tell them Steve from ABTA sent you.

You can also often find used copies of out-of-print books at **www.amazon.com.**

The Art of Raising a Puppy, by the Monks of New Skete, Little Brown & Co.

After the success of *How to Be Your Dog's Best Friend* (see later), everyone waited eagerly for the next book from the Monks of New Skete. Almost no trainer I know was disappointed when in 1991 *The Art of Raising a Puppy* was published. This book contains relatively mild compulsion methods. An excellent book for trainers who wish to more fully understand early developmental periods, excellent problem-solving techniques, good puppy obedience methods and general information. A must-read.

Behavior Problems in Dogs, by William E. Campbell, Behavior Today

Although some of the problem solutions in this book are a little unusual, *Behavior Problems in Dogs* remains one of the best single volumes on the subject in print. The book addresses everything from pica to house breaking. What is pica? Read the book. A must-read for serious problem solvers.

The Complete Dog Book, by the American Kennel Club, Howell Book House

Quite simply an invaluable reference guide. This book profiles every recognized American Kennel Club breed, giving history, standards and temperaments. It also has excellent general information on health and nutrition. A must for serious trainers.

Culture Clash, by Jean Donaldson, James and Kenneth

This book explains, in simple terms, how to more effectively communicate with your best friend. It is easy to read and understand, and contains a wealth of information.

DogPerfect, by Sarah Hodgson, Howell Book House
This is an excellent all-around book on training. Hodgson is an outstanding communicator and excellent trainer. Her methods are sensible, easy to understand and effective.

Dog Problems, by Carol Lea Benjamin, Howell Book House
An excellent problem-solving book. Although most trainers understand that to be effective in solving behavior problems you must first understand the root causes of the specific problem you wish to solve, understanding is still only the first step. Then we need methods. Methods abound in this book. It's worth reading.

Dog Training: The Gentle Modern Method, by David Weston, Howell Book House*
An outstanding little book for those trainers who wish to learn noncompulsion obedience techniques. Very creative, very well written.

DogWise, by John Fisher, Souvenir Press
This is an excellent book about basic obedience that uses noncompulsion methods. As more and more trainers shift to these types of techniques, it becomes more critical for a serious professional to master this style of training.

Don't Shoot the Dog, by Karen Pryor, Bantam Books
For those trainers who really want to understand more about the principles of behavior modification, this is your book. Absolutely a must-read. There are some trainers who insist it is the best training book out there.

How to Be Your Dog's Best Friend, by the Monks of New Skete, Little Brown & Co.
When this book was first published, everyone said "the monks of where?" No one had heard of these people. Since that time much has changed. *How to Be Your Dog's Best Friend* is an extremely well written, valuable training book. This book contains relatively mild

compulsion methods. It contains excellent problem-solving techniques and good solid obedience methods, as well. A must-read. This book has just been re-released with new, updated material. Once again, the Monks do not disappoint.

Mother Knows Best: The Natural Way to Train Your Dog, by Carol Lea Benjamin, Howell Book House

When it was first published in 1985, *Mother Knows Best* was one of the books that influenced numerous trainers to seriously look at non-compulsion training methods, especially with puppies. Although this book does contain relatively mild compulsion methods, it is very important reading for trainers who wish to understand how to train off leash without force. Definitely worth reading.

The New Knowledge of Dog Behavior, by Clarence Pfaffenberger, Dogwise Publishing

This book explains the critical developmental periods in a puppy's life, as well as some of the causes of adult canine problem behaviors. Based on the research performed by Drs. Scott and Fuller for their ground-breaking book *Genetics and the Social Behavior of the Dog, The New Knowledge of Dog Behavior* is an invaluable tool for those trainers who are serious about understanding developmental periods and how they relate to training.

Puppies For Dummies, by Sarah Hodgson, Wiley

Another excellent all-around training book by Hodgson. This one focuses on puppies: how to raise them and train them.

Teaching Dog Obedience Classes, by Joachim Volhard and Gail Tamases Fisher, Howell Book House*

For those instructors who are serious about improving their group obedience classes, this book has something for everyone. We have spoken to trainers with more than 30 years' experience teaching obedience classes who learned something from reading this book. Outstanding for rookie or veteran. A must read.

Other Reading Suggestions

Dog Language: An Encyclopedia of Canine Behavior, by Roger Abrantes, Wakan Tanka Press

The Evans Guide for Counseling Dog Owners, by Job Michael Evans, Howell Book House*

Family Dog, by Richard Wolters, E.P. Dutton*

Man Meets Dog, by Konrad Lorenz, Routledge Classics

Natural Health for Dogs and Cats, by Richard and Susan Pitcairn, Rodale Press

Of Wolves and Men, by Barry Holstun Lopez, Touchstone Books

The Right Dog for You, by Daniel F. Tortora, Fireside Press

Training Your Dog: The Step by Step Manual, by Joachim Volhard and Gail Tamases Fisher, Howell Book House

The Wolf, by L. David Mech, University of Minnesota Press

Why Does Your Dog Do That?, by Goran Bergman, Howell Book House*

INDEX